WILLIAM

james

THOUGHT IN THE ACT
A series edited by Erin Manning and Brian Massumi

WILLIAM James

EMPIRICISM AND PRAGMATISM

DAVID LAPOUJADE

Translated, and with a preface and afterword, by
THOMAS LAMARRE

Duke University Press   Durham and London   2020

English translation © 2020 David Lapoujade
The original French edition was published in 1997
by Presses Universitaires de France.
Preface and Afterword © 2020 Duke University Press
Cover design by Aimee Harrison
Text design by Courtney Leigh Baker
Typeset in Minion Pro by Westchester Publishing Services

Library of Congress Cataloging-in-Publication Data

Names: Lapoujade, David, author. | LaMarre, Thomas [date],
        translator, writer of supplementary textual content.
        Title: William James, empiricism and pragmatism /
    David Lapoujade ; translated and with a preface and afterword
by Thomas Lamarre
Other titles: William James, empirisme et pragmatisme. English
Description: Durham : Duke University Press, 2020. |

    Series: Thought in the act | Includes bibliographical references
    and index.
Identifiers: LCCN 2019013459 (print)
LCCN 2019016275 (ebook)
ISBN 9781478007593 (ebook)
ISBN 9781478005155 (hardcover)
ISBN 9781478006763 (pbk.)
Subjects: LCSH: James, William, 1842–1910. | Empiricism. |
    Pragmatism.
Classification: LCC B945.J24 (ebook) | LCC B945.J24 L36513 2020
    (print) | DDC 191—dc23
LC record available at https://lccn.loc.gov/2019013459

Cover photograph: "William James (1842–1910) sitting with Mrs.
Walden in Séance," n.d. Photograph by "Miss Carter." MS Am 1092
(1185), Houghton Library, Harvard University.

Contents

A Note on References

References to works of William James are from *The Works of William James*, electronic edition (Charlottesville, VA: InteLex, 2008), which is based on *The Works of William James*, edited by Frederick H. Burkhardt, Fredson Bowers, and Ignas K. Skrupskelis, 19 volumes (Cambridge, MA: Harvard University Press, 1975–1988).

References to James's correspondence are from *The Correspondence of William James*, electronic edition (Charlottesville, VA: InteLex, 2008), which is based on *The Correspondence of William James*, edited by Ignas K. Skrupskelis and Elizabeth M. Berkeley, with Bernice Grohskopf and Wilma Bradbeer, 12 volumes (Charlottesville: University Press of Virginia, 1992–2004).

Preface
Thomas Lamarre

First published in 1997, David Lapoujade's introduction to the philosophy William James anticipated a major shift in French thought, reinvigorating a dialogue between philosophical traditions that had been too neatly demarcated into territories—the Anglo-American tradition versus the Continental tradition, or British empiricism versus French rationalism, or analytic philosophy versus the Kantian legacy. The renewal of this dialogue between philosophical traditions is associated in North America with the work of Gilles Deleuze, where Deleuze's passing characterization of his philosophy as "transcendental empiricism," in combination with his brief but favorable accounts of James and Alfred North Whitehead, eventually inspired a closer look at both James and Whitehead.

Something similar was happening in intellectual circles in France. In Isabelle Stengers's majestic opus *Thinking with Whitehead*, first published in 2002, she expresses her preference for Whitehead over James, yet James is clearly a key thinker for her.[1] References to James's philosophy became increasingly evident in thinkers such as Bruno Latour as well. Impossible, then, to ignore the letters exchanged between Henri Bergson and James confirming the profound connections between their approaches. By the time Lapoujade's introduction was reissued in 2007, a veritable wave of James-related philosophy was unfurling. In 2008, Lapoujade published his monograph on William and Henry James, *Fictions du pragmatisme: William et Henry James* (Fictions of Pragmatism: William and Henry James), and a major monograph on William James by Stéphane Madelrieux appeared in the same year.[2] New essays reconsidering the dialogue between Bergson and James were also on the horizon, such as *Bergson et James: Cent an après* (2011).[3] In addition, Lapoujade's volume on Bergson, *Puissances du temps: Versions de Bergson* (*Powers of*

Time: Versions of Bergson), which came out in 2010, abounds in James-ian inspiration.[4]

While this new current of thought eventually gravitated toward connections between James and Whitehead and reinvigorated the dialogue between Bergson and James, such connections and dialogues gained traction in the context of a broader transformation in philosophical thinking. These new foci emerged within a new intellectual environment, itself emerging under the influence of theoretical developments in diverse fields, notably in the fields of science and technology studies and in media studies, where references to James are becoming as common as references to Deleuze, Guattari, Latour, and Stengers.

The power of Lapoujade's introduction to William James, still palpable more than twenty years after its initial publication, lies in its articulation of a truly Jamesian manner of thinking. While Lapoujade offers careful readings of the full range of James's work, his goal is not presentation, explication, or exegesis, which tend to impose external limits on a philosophy. His aim is to reveal the inner movement of Jamesian thought, to move with it, to work through its method. Much as Deleuze formulated Bergsonism, or a Bergsonian way of thinking, Lapoujade offers us a Jamesian turn of thought.

In *The Varieties of Religious Experience*, William James offers a succinct formulation of his method. He writes, "To understand a thing rightly we need to see it both out of its environment and in it, and to have acquaintance with the whole range of its variations."[5] It is precisely this method that enables Lapoujade to make his introduction to James a Jamesian movement of thought, in the process utterly transforming what we thought we knew about James.

True to James's method, Lapoujade begins with extraction. James is dug out of the environment in which his work has gradually become entrenched—the lineage of pragmatism, the discipline of American philosophy. Lapoujade thus opens with a challenge to those formulations of pragmatism, notably those of Richard Rorty, which circumscribe James's thought, restricting it to Americanized territory. The first gesture, then, is to consider James outside this Americanized territory, to counter this territorialization of James. In the name of radical empiricism, Lapoujade unearths and unroots James. The goal of such excavation is not, however, to purify the thing, to unify radical empiricism by reference to some transcendent position outside it. On the contrary, as Lapoujade remarks, *"wrong correspondences and ill adaptations which are precisely what make it function"*

"Each thing that we attempt to pry loose bears with it a halo of connections, its region." The second move, then, leads to an up-close view of what
is excavated, to consider how it all holds together. When thus isolated and
magnified, radical empiricism turns out to be a set of functions with connections among them that allow the set to hold together (instead of a rationally unified object). In this way, Lapoujade comes "to have acquaintance
with the full range of variations" of radical empiricism. This is also how
Lapoujade demonstrates that radical empiricism is not over and done. He
pursues it in the making, where series appear, variants yet to come.

There is another, pragmatic phase to the Jamesian movement of thought:
taking another look at the thing in its environment. As James writes of the
saint, "We must judge him not sentimentally only, and not in isolation,
but using our own intellectual standards, placing him in his environment,
and estimating his total function."[6] Thus Lapoujade offers another look
at the Jamesian thing, in its environment. But after Lapoujade has explored the full range of variations of radical empiricism, the environment
in which he resituates James is profoundly different from the Americanized territory of Rorty. Lapoujade arrives at another America, a world of
nomadic labor and spiritual movements, of vast open spaces crisscrossed
with networks of communication and transportation.

In keeping with James's defiant stance toward nationalism and imperialism, Lapoujade's Jamesian take on America is not a utopian vision. It does
not envision unity coming to this land in contractual, rational terms, or
even in ethnic and linguistic terms. What Lapoujade brings into view are
transitions related to material flows, which arise where networks of communication and transportation do not mesh smoothly, where their inter-
face implies gaps. Such transitions make for a patchwork holding-together
alongside the rationalized networks. This is also where nomadic workers
live, in transition. This is where those deemed mentally ill are forced to abide.
This is also where spiritual and political movements arise. For communities
of interpretation arise precisely where some sort of "wrong correspondence"
is felt, which must be navigated empirically and pragmatically. The Jamesian
America unearthed by Lapoujade is one of wrong correspondences and ill
adaptations, which are precisely what make it function.

This Jamesian way of seeing America is not calculated to be a neutral
description of a place over there, at a safe distance, or in the distant past,
to be considered as fundamentally incommensurable with, say, France.
Lapoujade's way of exploring claims to a territory is in keeping with

James's claim that some forms of knowledge cannot be carried out in neutral or rational fashion. James insists there are forms of knowledge that demand us to meet the object halfway. To meet James halfway, Lapoujade must to some extent pry himself loose from his environment. As such, the dialogue between what is called American philosophy and what is called French philosophy does not take place in some stripped down, objectivized, comparative space. Instead, what communicate are the wrong correspondences that run through each thing and its environment, holding the whole together. What communicate are the variations, which Lapoujade styles as the "halo of connections" or "region." The dialogue, then, takes place through variant series, as if we were reading two stories about the same event recounted from different perspectives. On James's side, for instance, may arise a "mosaic" series, with edged pieces and conjunctions. A variant series occurs on Lapoujade's side, an "archipelago" series, with disjunctive regions and halos. Where the mosaic series meets the archipelago series, terms change direction, taking on new conceptual force. The series meet halfway, becoming variant series.

These procedures based on variant series are also of great interest from the point of view of translation. The Jamesian turn in Lapoujade's thought involves a good deal of translation from English into French. The process is, in a sense, reversed in the present translation. Here, James in French is "returned" to English, while Lapoujade's French is translated into English. It becomes evident, however, that the initial process of translation was not linear and reversible to begin with. As a term is pried loose of its environment, something of its prior environment clings to it, even in the new environment. Of course, such effects may be muted or deadened. Keeping such effects alive is integral to Lapoujade's manner of thinking, however. The result is not a blurring of distinctions between the two languages, but a keener sense of their distinctions, which keeps them in communication through differences that remain nonconscious, imperceptible. French does not come to resemble English, any more than English starts to look or sound French. But a strange sense of their affinity arises, as if yet another language, yet another region, were in the offing. Their relation is one of semblance. The present translation strives to prolong such semblance: even as the passages by James are ostensibly returned to their original, this translation tries to sustain the entangled semblance that happens through Lapoujade's articulation of Jamesian concepts in French, but in the now English environment. What enters translation is neither one language nor the other, but both. Between the two arises the dark precursor, the uncanny intercessor.

There is precedent for such procedures in James. Famously, in *The Varieties of Religious Experience*, James presents his personal battle with depression and his spiritual crisis as those of an unnamed French correspondent, whose words he has translated into English for his audience.[7] It is possible to construe his gesture in a number of ways. Perhaps he is addressing those in the audience who already know him intimately, who understand that the experience is his. Perhaps his gesture constitutes a return of the repressed; precisely what he does not want to avow openly, he presents in an encrypted form. Both interpretations are possible, but there is a broader one. In James's bid to present his experience through translation between French and English is an oscillation between anonymous and personal experience, between reality and fiction. James tries to generate an experience of semblance, an uncanny experience, resonant with the experiences of sick souls, madness, and exceptional states, which put us in touch with transversal forces.

Likewise, Lapoujade, in the wake of his discovery of variant series through James, would explore in his next book, *Fictions of Pragmatism*, the relation between the James brothers. At the outset, he proposes, "The world of the brothers James is above all a world of relations."[8] Extracting the brothers from the separate territories in which they have usually been placed, Lapoujade is able to take a closer look at the full range of their variations. At the same time, when he "returns" them to their initial environment, that environment is a changed world. Now the two brothers are like coauthors of a single oeuvre, variant series within an ensemble, a world of relations. Thus, Lapoujade succeeds in looking at their differences differently, distributing them otherwise: "The entire oeuvre of the James brothers is built on [the] difference between direct relations and indirect relations. Indeed, above and beyond what they have in common, it may be what so profoundly differentiates the work of the philosopher from that of the novelist."[9]

The Jamesian turn applies to Lapoujade as well. As a student of Deleuze, he is commonly situated within a Deleuzian environment. Indeed, his introduction to William James has been widely hailed for its Deleuzian reading of James. Yet the Jamesian movement within Lapoujade's thought invites us to uproot him from "his" Deleuzian environment, to consider the full range of his philosophical variations. His masterful account of Deleuze's philosophy, *Deleuze, les movement aberrants* (2014), translated as

Aberrant Movements: The Philosophy of Gilles Deleuze (2017), then appears in a different light. Is Lapoujade's account of Deleuze not as Jamesian as his account of James is Deleuzian?

Ultimately, however, Lapoujade's thought is not best construed as Deleuzian or Jamesian. Nor is it to be understood primarily as a philosophy of relations, as pragmatism, or as a concatenation of radical and transcendental empiricism. It is above all about thinking across variations and series, about variant series, about exploring the full range of variations with an eye to the emergence of new worlds and regions—regions of experience whose conceptual and geopolitical contours do not correspond to those on our received philosophical maps.

William James is best remembered for contributing to psychology the famous phrase "stream of consciousness," and for establishing the doctrine of pragmatism, principally through his instrumentalist theory of truth: "Our account of truth is an account of truths in the plural . . . having only this quality in common, that they *pay.* . . . Truth for us is simply a collective name for verification-processes, just as health, wealth, strength, etc., are names for other processes connected with life, and also pursued because it pays to pursue them."[1] Truth is what brings a return, what "pays"; it is about favorable actions that succeed. A simple reversal of this phrase is enough to make pragmatism look like nothing more than a caricature of the symbols of American-style success: health, wealth, strength are the sole truths.

The work of James is often seen as a philosophy of unfettered capitalism, with ideas that pay, truths that "live on credit," that is, everything that might commonly be taken for "pragmatism" today, as a sort of capitalist ready-made. Max Horkeimer, for instance, thus denounces pragmatism from Charles S. Peirce to John Dewey: "Their philosophy reflects, with an almost disarming candor, the spirit of the prevailing business culture."[2] Great effort has gone into drawing an image of a specifically American philosophy—direct, naïve, mercantile—of which James's pragmatism would be the liveliest incarnation. Oddly, the idea of a properly American philosophy is more commonly invoked when it comes to James than to his contemporaries, such as Peirce or Josiah Royce. James is presented as the one who gives America its national philosophy, much as James Fenimore Cooper and Walt Whitman are said to provide its literature.

Yet nothing could be further from James than the recent "neo-pragmatist" theses of Rorty, for instance, who proposes to establish specifically American criteria for universal democratic conversation, and to promote the

United States as an indigenous source of fundamental values. Nothing could be less pluralist or less in keeping with James's thought (or with Dewey's), despite Rorty's claims to follow it. James's efforts to clear up such misunderstandings have come to naught: pragmatism remains the philosophy of the American businessman, and the term no longer holds any meaning other than opportunistic action. Yet it was none other than William James who denounced, time and again, the imperialist ambitions of the United States, its generalized mercantilism, and its cult of money and financial success.[3]

Nor is James's pragmatism a "philosophy of action," in the sense of aiming to establish a theory of action, or describing which of its mechanisms make for greater efficiency, or in the sense of constantly calling on action as an ultimate end. The alleged "let us be practical" does not mean that everything will have to work out, at any cost, regardless of underlying conditions, provided a satisfactory return is had. The pragmatic definition of truth does not come down to validation through action, even if James maintains that the truth of an idea lies partly in its "practical consequences." His interpreters persistently identify the field of practice with the domain of action. Yet, for James, the term "practical" does not necessarily refer to the domain of action as opposed to the field of theoretical reflection; it refers above all to a point of view: "practical" means that reality, thought, knowledge (and also action) are considered in terms of their making. In a general way, James's philosophy is a philosophy of how humans are made in a world that is itself also being made. The reason he objects to rationalists and absolutists (especially the Hegelians, even though they were the first to introduce movement into concepts) comes of how they step in too late, after things have happened, "when a form of life has grown old," and the world has put forth everything it may put forth. As James says, "What really *exists* is not things made but things in the making."[4] Any reality is to be considered in the moment of its creating. Nonetheless this gesture should not be construed as making for a philosophy of the self-made man (that is, individualism, of which some have accused him), for it is evident that the individual could not be made if she were not at the same time caught up in tremendous flows of the world, traversed by the incessant movement of what is in the making. This problem is one that runs through all of James's philosophy: How can knowledge, truth, and belief be made if the world in which we live is open to perpetual novelty? Thus, for instance, it is not enough to say that an idea is thought within the mind, or that the mind represents an idea. Such a definition is deprived of movement and, in this respect, is largely incomplete; what must be demonstrated is how the idea is made in the mind, and how the mind is made by it. What must be introduced into its definition is what James calls "practical consequences," essentially pragmatic criteria. The idea is defined no longer as a representation or modification of the mind but as a process by which mind is made.

Key advances in psychology around the years 1880–90 had already introduced such an approach.[5] In *Principles of Psychology*, psychological realities are treated as a veritable mishmash of intertwining and interpenetrating flows. Consciousness is not defined as a substantial reality, nor even as a reflexive act; consciousness is the movement of what is being made conscious. Such work shows, in effect, how consciousness never stops marking its limits within thought, how consciousness expands or contracts away from the unconscious bordering it.

James later (around 1904) takes up the same question but considerably enlarges it when he inaugurates "radical empiricism," introducing the notion of pure experience. Now it is a matter of showing that a plane of thought exists that precedes all the categories of psychology and traditional philosophy, and that those categories, far from being constitutive, must, on the contrary, be constituted on the basis of this plane of thought. Subject and object, matter and thought, are described not as givens or a priori forms but as processes that are being made within thought or alongside it. Freeing the movement of what is in the making on the psychological plane, as on the philosophical plane, invariably implies a critique of the forms in which we usually tend to partition flows of life, thought, and matter.

If empiricism is, strictly speaking, James's philosophy, what are we to make of pragmatism? Pragmatism is not a philosophy. It is a method, nothing other than a method, of which the general maxim, borrowed from Peirce, is as follows: "There is no distinction of meaning so fine as to consist in anything but a possible difference of practice."[6] It is true that James, from 1907, gives a double definition to pragmatism that allows us to think that it is something other than a simple method: "Such then would be the scope of pragmatism—first, a method; and second, a genetic theory of what is meant by truth."[7] Yet this theory is an effect of the method itself and is thus inseparable from it. Now we may begin to clarify these two aspects of pragmatism.

In the first instance, pragmatism is a method of practical evaluation. It examines ideas, concepts, and philosophies, not from the point of view of their internal coherence or their rationality but as a function of their "practical consequences." We have to evaluate ideas in light of how they propose to make us act or think. It all comes down to the following question: What makes possible the truth of our ideas? Or, how does an idea become true? How is a true idea made? Thus, in the second instance, the pragmatic method is inseparable from a tool of construction (or a genetic theory of what is meant by truth, to use James's turn of phrase). Pragmatism thus responds to the question of how to produce ideas for acting or thinking. The only thing it can do, as a method of evaluation, is to help us choose, from among philosophies, religions, and social ideas, those that are most beneficial to our action or thought. For example, it is odd that we can equally well characterize the same world in terms of generalized determinism as in terms of sovereign free will, as if this changed nothing. Yet, if we can in theory choose indifferently between determinism and free will, such is not the case in practice. Our action is not the same if we support the one or the other. Pragmatism is not a philosophy but a method for choosing among philosophies. As a tool for construction, however, what it must do is to help us create ideas that may be of use in acting or thinking. As such, it becomes a tool of creation. *How are ideas made, and what do we do with ideas?*—these are two axes of the pragmatic method. In general terms, pragmatism conceives of ideas as spurs for action, which allow us to create and evaluate. This is where things get difficult: it is not a method about creating but a method for creating.

These two inseparable aspects of pragmatism echo two expressions that often overlap in James: reality is made; reality is in the making. There is a sort of moral exigency to becoming: the world is in the making at the same time that it has to be made. This means that action, far from being a solution, has become a problem. Acting and thinking are now problems insofar as they entail risk. "In the total game of life we stake our persons all the while."[8] Of course, not all our actions or thoughts entail risk; yet, before turning into settled habits, they initially involved experimentation. This is the moment that interests James. Speaking generally, pragmatism is addressed to someone who, in some area or another, is no longer capable of acting, precisely someone for whom acting constitutes a problem or a risk. You cannot take risks, however, unless you have *faith*.

Such a theme is not original to James. Transcendentalism already invoked it as an essential condition.[9] It insistently called on faith. The individual must be the pioneer who has faith in himself, in his strength, in his judgment, just as he has faith in the power of Nature with which he is unified in a feeling of fusion (even if it entails distrust of conformism within society and the city, as with Emerson as well as with Thoreau when he calls for "civil disobedience"). Faith is inseparable from a Romantic union with the Whole. As Emerson says in *Self-Reliance*, the prayer of the farmer kneeling in his field to weed is heard throughout nature.[10] He enters into communion with the all-encompassing unity of the Over-Soul. There is thus no faith in self without faith in human beings, in all humanity, in nature, and in God. Such a great circular trinity, Divinity-Nature-Humanity, is also found in another great transcendentalist, William James's father Henry James Sr.[11]

There is no doubt that, in some respects, pragmatism is a prolongation of transcendentalism. Like transcendentalism, pragmatism calls for individual action, for risk, and for faith. A fundamental break nonetheless occurs: it is no longer possible to maintain the great fusional harmony between Humans, Nature, and God. To give but one example, as James remarks, when you consider the development of sciences, in the plural, and the disorder and indetermination they introduce into the structure of our universe, the existence of a single God whose archetypes we copy becomes difficult to believe in. Pluralism breaks fusional unity much as Darwinism broke harmonic finality. The previous sort of naïveté and confident optimism is no longer possible for us moderns. James makes a similar observation, but on another plane, when in *The Varieties of Religious Experience* he describes numerous cases in which belief collapses, in which an individual is no longer capable of belief, not only in God or in ideals, but also in himself and in the very world that lies before him. When we go through such crises, the world suddenly loses all meaning. The diverse connections that bind us to the world break, one after the other. In sum, we can no longer believe as we did before; action becomes impossible because we have lost faith.

Pragmatism is born of such observations. It is not the triumphant echo of America but, on the contrary, the symptom of a profound break that ruptures the wholeness of action. It does not follow the movement of what is in the making without struggling against the movement of what is being unmade. It is in this sense that action is a problem for James, and not in the least a universal solution. James's diagnostic is akin to that of Nietzsche: we no longer believe in anything. Nietzsche diagnoses it through the symptom of nihilism, primarily in the "nothingness of will" of active nihilism. James diagnoses it in the profound loss of faith that translates into a profound crisis of action. The one who no longer believes, the one who no longer has faith, remains immobile and without reaction, *undone*. She is as if stricken with a death of the senses.[12] Of course, we continue to act as we always do, and undoubtedly even with a considerable "return," but do we still believe in our actions? With what intensity? Do we still believe in the world that makes us act? How can we feel faith in others, have faith in ourselves, and even have faith in the world? Which philosophy, which doctrine, will restore our faith? Such questions are so many subsets of the central problem.

The task of philosophy is thus not to seek the true or the rational, but to give us reasons to believe in this world just as the religious person is disposed to find reasons to believe in another world. The pragmatic method is inseparable from this general problem. When James asks, "What is a true idea?" he really means, "What are the signs in which one can have faith?" For, ultimately, it is never signs in general in which we do or don't place our faith—but specific signs, which the pragmatic method allows us to find. For instance, others express themselves through signs, and yet we must have signs other than those they explicitly manifest if we are to know whether we can believe in what they say. The signs by which I understand what someone says are not the same as those by which I believe in what someone says. Likewise when we say that we no longer believe in this world: this really means that we cease to believe in certain signs that constitute its existence for us. In other words, pragmatism requires a new theory of signs.

Pragmatism is not a philosophy, but it demands with its every fiber a philosophy that permits us to act once again, not a philosophy in which we can believe, but rather a philosophy that makes us believe. There is no lack of ideas in which to believe and on which to act—God, Self, Revolution, Progress—but something is broken in our power to believe. And it remains broken unless the pragmatic method of evaluation makes clear to us that pluralism, more than any other philosophy, provides us with motives for action. The question then becomes: What is it exactly about pluralism that makes us act? And correlatively, what is about other philosophies that they do not produce such an effect?

The paradox is that James sees in pluralism the form most capable of restoring such belief, while other thinkers, on the contrary, see in it pure and simple relativism, the form that generates all our skepticisms. Is it not the plurality of spaces in geometry that makes us doubt the truth of axioms, and the plurality of philosophies that makes us doubt the truth of each doctrine, and so forth? Why the form of pluralism? Someone who affirms the existence of a single truth, of a single science, of a single dogma, whom James calls the "absolutist," he too believes. He believes more fervently than the pluralist. Why then claim that pluralism is the most capable of making us believe when, on the contrary, it gives us more reasons for doubt than does absolutism? It is imperative to try to resolve this question: How does the pluralism of radical empiricism foster faith (when it is presumed to engender doubt and suspicion)? Put another way, how do we make pluralism in general an object of faith?

We should not, for all that, presume that James's philosophy was for him a means of "getting out" of psychology. Pragmatism also needs a psychology. James's thought is always defined as pluralism, and this pluralism as perspectivism. To each consciousness, taken in itself, the question is posed of how to believe and act. In this sense, the pragmatic method may be defined with good reason as "democratic."[13] It cannot dictate a universal rule. Such a stance makes clear why pragmatism needs a psychology, since it examines the effect produced by ideas on a consciousness. Yet this way of putting it is still too general. It does not address what is specifically of concern: Why is it that the problem of faith requires a psychology of consciousness conceived in terms of flow?

By definition, flow never ceases to vary, to pass through dips and rises, and the field of consciousness corresponding to these variations never stops expanding and contracting. Thus a consciousness believes and acts when the variations that traverse it cross a certain threshold—whence a psychology that studies variations of the field of consciousness, a psychology of intensity. Now, in *The Varieties of Religious Experience*, James shows that a field of consciousness enlarges and expands its connections as a function of the extent of its faith. This means that variations in intensity of consciousness are nothing other than variations in the feeling of faith. It is a psychology of faith or, if one prefers, for the problem of faith. In this way, far from being independent of pragmatism, such a psychology is the only one possible for the general problem that James poses, for which he must find a solution: What does a consciousness need for signs to have a meaning? Or in other words: What is needed for signs to spur consciousness to action? Which is, in still other words, the same as asking: What is needed for signs to lead a consciousness to produce other signs, actions, or thoughts in connection with the first ones? In this summary form, three distinct axes emerge: pragmatism, whose problem consists of determining which signs or ideas lead to our being able to act or to augment our power to act; radical empiricism, whose problem consists of determining how signs are constituted and the rules according to which they are organized; and to a lesser extent, psychology, whose problem consists of determining what allows consciousness to give meaning to the signs it perceives and how consciousness responds to them through variations in its flow. These are the three problems that we must attempt to resolve.

RADICAL EMPIRICISM

1

Plane and Material: Pure Experience

One of the essential features of empiricism in general involves the construction of a plane that allows for observing how excesses, beliefs, judgments, and so forth are made. Experience is observed based on a sort of pure experience, a first moment of *inexperience*—the blank slate. For classical empiricists like John Locke and David Hume, this plane remains inextricable from human ignorance or a newborn's lack of knowledge, when the mind is still but a disparate set of psychic atoms without connections among them. Thus Hume asks whether someone *who has never seen water* can infer from its fluidity and transparency that it will suffocate him.[1] Rather than interpreting this artifice in terms of a battle between innatism and Cartesianism, we should think of it in terms of establishing a new method. Of course the Cartesian method of doubt also lies in producing a tabula rasa of all forms of knowledge; the force of doubt, however, appears like the negative flipside of the basic certainty that has not yet been discovered but already awaits, concealed—the "I think." Put another way, Cartesianism does not truly entail a blank slate since it allows the "I think" an existence outside it; "I think" devises the blank slate and determines its finality. The advantage of the empiricist method is that it does not allow for anything outside. It begins with a plane where nothing is preestablished, where no form of knowledge, no certainty—even virtual—has yet appeared, such that everything has the right to be constructed.

In James's psychology, everything begins in the manner of classical empiricism. He calls this moment of inexperience "pure experience." At the time he wrote *Principles of Psychology* (1890), pure experience was applicable to all states without consciousness. Examples are the sensations of newborns, comatose states, hallucinations induced by certain drugs—in short, any state in which distinctions are not yet made or cease to be made. If psychology only begins with the reflexive movement of introspection, then such states mark the limit of psychological investigation as such. "This stage of reflective condition is, more or less explicitly, our habitual adult state of mind. *It cannot, however, be regarded as primitive.* The consciousness of objects must come first. We seem to lapse into this primordial condition when consciousness is reduced to a minimum by the inhalation of anaesthetics or during a faint."[2] What makes such states so difficult to access analytically is that they immerse us in a sort of "vague monism" in which we no longer distinguish subject and object, while the psychologist remains adamantly dualist. "It supposes two elements, mind knowing and thing known, and treats them as irreducible."[3] The psychologist only intervenes as such when consciousness has already been distinguished from the object that consciousness posits before it, that is, when the object is known. The "empiricist" thus comes prior to—and grounds—the natural psychologist who is intent on describing the fact of consciousness in its duality. The empiricist tells us about the impersonal ground that consciousness comes from, without being able to say anything about it.

Such descriptions have their limits. By the time psychology steps in, pure experience is only accessible as always already lost. If we say that it is an experience without consciousness, psychology takes the expression in the most literal manner; it seeks the fact: at a sensory level, it is not possible to establish any distinction between consciousness and its object, either because consciousness is not yet there (the newborn), or because it is no longer there (fainting, drugs). Thus experience is pure because the one who has it is pure. Put another way, the plane is always reduced to a moment that is swiftly surpassed (and is embodied in theoretical characters, and fleeting ones at that); psychology is no more capable than classical empiricism of deriving a genuine plane from these moments, which is to say, of establishing a reality copresent with all the data happening in it.

In other words, psychology does not have a genetic field at its disposal: either it traces backward toward pure experience as toward a limit yet encounters states too inconsistent to build its geneses, or it intervenes when everything is already constituted and has no other choice than to make do with already constituted geneses. It makes sense that Kant and Edmund Husserl, although guided by very different motivations, seek to constitute a transcendental field beyond all psychology. In effect, the domain of the transcendental frees up a field that allows for the constitution of true geneses because the field has first been purified of its empirical material and of the naïvetés of psychological naturalism. We may go back to the pure conditions tied together by a transcendental ego to constitute a plane; thus Husserl may claim to have truly attained pure experience: "Its beginning is the pure—and, so to speak, still dumb—psychological experience, which now must be made to utter its own sense with no adulteration. The truly first utterance, however, is the Cartesian utterance of the *ego cogito*."[4] Oddly, however, no sooner does he reach this plane than he finds the same problem that is encountered in Descartes: the ego does not of itself make for the object of a genesis since it is, on the contrary, the condition of law. "Pure" means precisely that lived experiences are studied insofar as they are immanent *to consciousness*. Transcendental philosophies free themselves well enough of empirical material yet nonetheless keep the forms inherited from psychology, even if they reorganize them to suit the requirements of their new domain.

If the ambition of James's thought is to seize reality in the moment of its making, he cannot adopt either of these two approaches. He will neither pursue the material geneses of psychology nor reconstruct the formal geneses of transcendental philosophies, for in both instances, even though every effort is made to follow the movement of what is in the making and to remain immanent to this movement, such efforts fail every time because the making is subjugated to preexisting forms that interrupt its very process. The real difficulty thus lies entirely in opening a third way, in establishing a pure experience that is not reducible to a pure sensory matter, nor constituted by forms of a pure subjectivity. What is needed are the fleeting moments described previously, which can constitute a true plane of construction.

This is what James attempts in *Essays in Radical Empiricism* (1904). In *Principles of Psychology* and subsequent texts, pure experience is only introduced within the framework of a psychological analysis or an epistemological description (which essentially means in terms of sensation). These latter texts present a significant overturning of the prior approach, proceeding in exactly the opposite direction: interpreting psychological analyses based on the field of pure experience. What becomes of subject, object, consciousness, and body from the point of view of pure experience? Dealing with them demands clearing the horizon of obstacles, to allow us to see how they are made.

What must be explored are the movements that are located beneath the forms of psychology or inherited from them. We have the feeling of witnessing the birth of a new world. James's entire enterprise lies in tracing back to what falls short of epistemological dualisms, back to where relations are given in a pure state, when they are not yet divided into any categorical binary whatsoever (subject/object; matter/spirit; and so forth). It is a matter of establishing a new point of view. If at one time pure experience was manifested locally and punctually, by way of certain interstices through which one caught a glimpse of chaos liberated by the matter of sensations (such as the dizziness of fainting or anesthesia), then, from now on, pure experience applies to whatever happens, to any event—of a fire burning, of a person reading in a train. It may even be applied to something entirely material, such as a chemical reaction. How is such an expansion possible?

The general principle of pure experience is as follows: "Nothing shall be admitted as fact, it says, except what can be experienced at some definite time by some experient; and for every feature of fact ever so experienced, a definite place must be found somewhere in the final system of reality."[5] Pure experience is, in a manner that remains to be defined, the universal That. It is the immense world of a nonqualified, neutral material. At the same time, it is "an immediate flow of life." Strictly speaking, we encounter nothing more of it than a bunch of "this" and "there." And such terms are only conventions for signifying that no qualifier, even as basic as "this" and "there," can designate this universe. None of the pure forms of transcendental philosophies are to be found. James sometimes uses the term "matter," but in the vague sense of stuff or materials. Unlike empirical matter, material designates a reality that can be at once physical and mental. Put another way, there is nothing purely mental or purely material; rather everything is composed of physical-mental material. James may thus say of consciousness, "There is, I mean, no aboriginal stuff or quality of being, contrasted with that of which material objects are made, out of which our thoughts of them are made."[6] This is a new version of vague monism.[7] Monism, however, is no longer a thinking of the All but of the interval, the in-between. It is a matter of an intermediary reality that stretches between mind and matter, precisely where they are closely merged, but on the basis of which they are distinguished as well, albeit only virtually.[8] We do not, properly speaking, yet make any distinction between them, and yet we never cease to make the distinction.

In other words, James gives material a genuine status, that of *plane*. He begins with the supposition that "there is only one primal stuff or material in the world, a stuff *of which everything is composed*, and . . . we call that stuff 'pure experience.'"[9] Pure does not here mean nonempirical; on the contrary, it is empirical, nothing but empirical. It is the datum in its pure state. It is no one's datum. It is given in itself. It is not yet given for anyone; it is a world in which neither subject nor object has yet appeared. In this sense, we may speak of radical empiricism. Experience is therefore to be expanded in a general sense: pure experience is the set of anything that is in relation with something else without consciousness of this relation necessarily being involved. Something of this usage of "experience" may be found in the French expression *faire une expérience*, or "to have an experience," which also means "to do an experiment," for instance, an experiment on the crystallization of sodium and chloride. We are the ones who do the experiment; but the experience does not apply to us, it applies to what is put into relation: it is, in fact, the sodium and chloride that crystallize; they do the experience of crystallization. Insofar as it is pure, experience may equally well apply to "subjects" as to "objects" (which is but a manner of speaking since neither subject nor object exists at this level).

Vague Monism: Experience without Ego

We are dealing with a situation in which nothing but relations stretch to the horizon, an expanse populated only with relative terms. There are relations precisely insofar as it is a question of a field of experiences. Experiences overlap and stretch out indefinitely, folding into one another, interpenetrating, sometimes without any assignable limit. The only "experiential" unities or "materials" are patches, fragments, or bits of experience, which is to say, just more relations. James often compares experience to fabric, but it is a fabric composed of patches.[10] Such is the neutral world prior to psychology, prior to consciousness. Pluralism and continuity are its two essential characteristics. It is a field on which neither subject nor object are yet differentiated, a world of pure movements. James clarifies, in terms much like Bergson's, "The entire field of experience turns out to be transparent through and through, or put together like a space entirely made of mirrors."[11]

As James's account is extended to address these broader points, the inspiration of Bergson's *Matter and Memory* appears quite evident. Indeed, in his masterful first chapter, Bergson describes a world unheard of, entirely made up of a primordial flow of images, each reflected in the others in a limitless mirroring.[12] Everything is image. Matter, body, brain are made of images. Yet, for Bergson as for James, these images are not for anyone. They are not images of things since "things" are also images. They are images in themselves.[13] The Bergsonian image corresponds to pure experience in James. Bergson replaces a system of mechanical causality with a system of optic refraction. A movement is a luminous propagation through a flow of matter that is also luminous, also in movement. There is transparency to matter: matter makes movement visible when it passes through a body also in movement. Image is defined as matter and movement. Image is not specifically mental, even if mental images are specific. "Only if, when we consider any other given place in the universe, we can regard the action of all matter as passing through it without resistance and without loss, and the photograph of the whole as translucent: here there is wanting behind the plate the black screen on which the image could be shown."[14]

Nonetheless James's descriptions, like those of Bergson, present an obvious difficulty. How can there be a pure experience or an image in itself? Should it not be supposed that the fragment of pure experience or the Bergsonian image require at the least someone to whom they appear? An experience that no one has, an image that is not represented to anyone, are these not pure impossibilities? Should we not presuppose at least a distinction between what has the experience and what the experience is made of—forms, however rudimentary, however larval, of subject and object? Does James not say that pure experience "is *conscious*, and it is *what we are conscious of*"?[15] It may well be thought that James and Bergson are pushing the terms "experience" and "image" too far; and yet it is in fact the philosophical tradition that uses them in too restrictive a manner, insofar as it relates them arbitrarily to a subject for whom image and experience exist. The implicit assumption, then, is that the subject is first, and all that is given is given to a subject. This is precisely what James and Bergson object to, the foundational and constituent subject, for as soon as the subject is given, a way out of it must be sought.

This is why the neutral character of experience becomes necessary, neutral in the sense that everything remains indefinite, and that material cannot be qualified as objective, subjective, as matter or mind. A field of indivisible events, whose repercussions and reverberations may later "divide," becomes a necessary point of departure. Pure experience is experience from the point of view of the event. The event arises at the intersection where subject and object meet (if that relation is privileged), and in their in-between, but before they are there: this is why the event is not their fusion; it comes before them. Subject and object are successors to it. The flaw of the subject/object division lies precisely in its implicit presupposition of two worlds, one of them doubling the other, or one of them ruling over the other. It stands to reason, then, that there is only one event because there is only one world.[16] Unity precedes and virtually contains its division. This is why, once again, the empiricism comes before the psychology, before the distinctions of transcendental philosophies—both de facto and de jure.

Is it possible that, contrary to expectations, when pushed to its limit, or "radicalized," empiricism may rediscover a transcendental inspiration? The "immediate flow of life" is the immanent condition for all experience. Affirming that everything boils down to experience before consciousness meets the requirements of transcendental inquiry in this respect. How else to describe radical empiricism if not in terms of the attainment of a new transcendental, a transcendental empiricism?[17] It may be objected that pure experience is already an experience, and as such, it must be constituted. But this is not true of experience in itself. We have only to ask, how is an experience in itself possible? For it is experience in itself that now makes possible any experience for any subject whatsoever. As such, experience in itself is truly a condition, even if the condition is obviously not a priori since it is already *of* experience. James thus proposes a complete reversal of perspective, which allows for the empirical and the transcendental to be identical.[18] In this way, James is not opposed to the idea of constructing a transcendental field; he is opposed to the idea that this field may be made to depend on a subject form. What is original and novel in James, as in Bergson, lies precisely in thinking that the field of pure experience is deployed for itself.

There are already hints of such a reversal in James's psychology. Contrary to what is often said, James begins not with the "stream of consciousness" but with a more radical given from which the stream of consciousness is derived. What psychology first encounters is an impersonal stream of thought. "*The first fact for us, then, as psychologists, is that thinking of some sort goes on. . . .* If we could say in English 'it thinks,' as we say 'it rains' or 'it blows,' we should be stating the fact most simply and with the minimum of assumption. As we cannot, we must simply say that *thought goes on.*"[19] The point of departure is not the ego but a neutral, indefinite event. The immanence of flow is not related directly to an ego, as is the case in Kant and in Husserl, who thus preserve more of psychology than they imagine. Of course, the constitution of the transcendental field allows them to empty psychology of its positive empirical core, but it does not allow them to free themselves of the categories of psychology, particularly those of the ego. Transcendental philosophies appear as stripped-down versions of psychology whose forms they heighten and duplicate.[20]

Kant and Husserl certainly purified forms of their empirical matter; but it is legitimate to ask: Why did they not extend this purification to the forms themselves? Is it possible to place forms within the transcendental field, without further scrutiny, without considering what commitments they entail? Psychology is reproached for its empiricism or naturalism when it would have been better to reproach it for extracting bad forms from them, *already constituted* forms. Isn't this exactly what James does when he proposes to treat consciousness and the brain as flows? Strictly speaking, psychology is not to be faulted for its empiricism and naturalism; it is to be faulted for making poor distinctions, for distorting descriptions, and, in short, for not knowing how to pursue material flows. Such an approach makes clear that, for Kant as for Husserl, forms are pure insofar as they are forms. Kant and Husserl stress beginning with forms and only forms, since a constituent role is reserved for them (by means of the a priori of any possible experience for Kant, and by means of the pure immanence of lived experience of consciousness for Husserl). This gesture entails a sort of Aristotelian or Thomist assumption to the effect that forms have de facto superiority over their materials.[21] James's hypothesis, however, shows that it is not possible to establish a transcendental field independently of psychology if a hylomorphic schema is preserved, in which priority is given to matter or to form. In other words, the matter-form couple is not suited to describing the movement of what is in the making.

Interpretation and Signifying Series

Maybe, with the world of pure experience, we have available to us a properly genetic plane, which will permit us to track this movement with precision. The world of pure experience is a world without subject or object, or rather a neutral world, that is developed and extended into the subject/object relationship; which means that pure experience "is *conscious*, and it is *what* we are conscious of"—at once, inseparably. From one point of view, it is neither subject nor object, neither mental nor physical, and from another point of view, it is both at once, simultaneously, albeit still virtually. As Bergson writes in his letter to James, "It is not actually presented to a consciousness."[22] The world of pure experience thus appears as a vast field replete with virtualities, "a *that* which is not yet any definite *what*, tho ready to be all sorts of whats."[23] It is on this plane that division takes place, and distinctions may be constructed. How is it then that an event is said to be subjective or objective? The question is no longer how to have a pure experience but, on the contrary, how experience ceases to be pure.

Pure experience no longer applies only to certain sensations (fainting, etc.); it applies to all experience. "Let the reader arrest himself in the act of reading this article now. *Now* this is a pure experience, a phenomenon, or datum, a mere *that* or content of fact. 'Reading' simply is, is there; and whether there for some one's consciousness, or there for physical nature, is a question not yet put."[24] We need to be precise: any experience is pure, but only at the neutral point of the present. "The instant field of the present is always experience in its 'pure' state."[25] Each conscious thought is just like the joint in a bamboo stem, tying together past and future in a single continuous present—what James calls "specious present"; but this also means that there exists a point of pure present whose thought does not belong to consciousness, or at least not yet, as if separated from it by the flow of temporal continuity.[26]

It is only later, when reflecting on what has happened, that the event is divided into a distinction between consciousness and its object. In the interval, a process of appropriation is carried out; the thought that follows is accomplished by the preceding thought, inheriting it; such is the retrospective act of appropriation of thought, even as it also tends toward the future. "Each pulse of cognitive consciousness, each Thought, dies away and is replaced by another. . . . Each Thought is thus born an owner, and dies owned, transmitting whatever it realized as its Self to its own later proprietor."[27] Thus the thought-event, the neutral and indefinite "thought goes on" described by psychology, becomes *my* thought, the thought of my consciousness, through a work of immediate retrospective appropriation that integrates it into prior thoughts—possesses it. It is a process of interpretation. To be conscious is to interpret the present still impersonal thought as mine.[28] No sooner does the act of possession occur than pure experience transforms and disappears as such; it enters into a perspective. The datum becomes *my* datum, constituted from a past in light of a future. Experience has become material for interpretation.

Interpreting is a matter of constructing series. Take the following event: an individual reading in a room. "What are the two processes, now, into which the room-experience simultaneously enters in this way? One of them is the reader's personal biography, the other is the history of the house of which the room is part. . . . The physical and the mental operations form curiously incompatible groups. As a room, the experience has occupied that spot and had that environment for thirty years. As your field of consciousness it may never have existed until now."[29] This is one and the same event, "reading in a room," which is primordially neutral but which *becomes* objective and subjective (if we wish to privilege this particular relation) following the series—"biography" or "history"—in which the event is integrated. Thus so-called objective and subjective series will be constituted. In this sense, interpreting consists of constructing and running through series.

We should not think, however, that this set of recursive processes consists of a simple return to self, that James renews traditional definitions of consciousness as a reflexive act in opposition to a flow of nonreflexive mindless thought. Still less should we assume that this movement takes recourse in a *self* that bestows meaning. James seems to be concerned with something else: either an event is considered in isolation, and it is then a matter of "pure experience," or the event is integrated into a series, and it changes in nature, it takes on meaning. To take up James's terms, something becomes some thing; that becomes a what. The process of signification begins with taking on series. In effect, the event by itself may well be a sign, but that would not be enough for it to take on meaning. One term will not suffice. Doesn't signification presuppose two terms, the sign and that to which it refers, as in the work of Ferdinand de Saussure, with the union of signifier and signified?[30] Yet, if the problem is posed in this way, we do not know how the sign signifies. Certainly, there is a signified, but it is not possible to specify what is entailed in signifying. The two terms are attached to each other, inseparable, yet we do not know how meaning is made.

The process of signification necessarily calls for a series with three terms, as the previous description of the process of appropriation suggests. A sign does not refer to a thing, even in a basic relationship of designation. Indeed it is necessary to know what is being signified of the thing, which aspect of it is targeted, the subjective aspect or the objective aspect. To specify it, the sign must first refer to a second sign within the thought, which interprets the first sign by relating it to the event that has some significance to it (because what an object can signify can never be signified in its totality), which is precisely a third term. In Peirce's terminology, a major source of inspiration for James, the second sign is called the interpretant of the first. It is under these conditions that the sign signifies, and the object is signified. A second sign (interpretant) always steps in to refer to a third term (the aspect of the object signified by the first). A sign does not signify because it relates to the object. It signifies through a sign that relates it to the object through what the object has of significance, which itself becomes a sign. In this way, to say that the thought-event signifies at once my thought (one) is only possible if the interpretant (two)—the emotion or the sense of belonging—captures this aspect of the event (three) for the interpretation to take on meaning. Herein lies the movement of possessing, but now defined as a semiotic process. There is nothing at all reflexive about it; on the contrary, it is a matter of an indefinitely open interpretative process, in accordance with its serial nature. As Peirce says, "There is no moment at which there is a thought belonging to this series, subsequently to which there is not a thought which interprets or repeats it. There is no exception, therefore, to the law that every thought-sign is translated or interpreted in a subsequent one," which means everything is a sign.[31] Objects and things are signs, and inversely, signs are things. To say that we pass from sign to sign means precisely this: we perceive things themselves. The passage from the subjective room to the objective room is but a passage from one series of signs to another, from one interpretation to another, while yet remaining within one and the same reality in signs.

It is clear at this juncture how interpretations come to populate the "neutral" desert of pure experience, introducing into it landmarks for the journey that is *an* experience. In effect, nothing other than interpretations can be found. From the point of view of radical empiricism, distinctions such as subject/object, thought/matter, and physical world/psychic world are but interpretations—nothing other than signs. "Thus, the properties of subject and object, represented and representation, thing and thought, signify a practical distinction, which is of extreme importance, but which is of a functional kind only, and in no way ontological as it has been represented in classical dualism."[32] But what then makes possible the reality of such experimentations if they are no longer anything but signs? It is a matter of belief, or rather, the emotional reaction provoked by the event—what makes us believe. "Real" is said of what triggers an emotion in us: "*In its inner nature, belief, or the sense of reality, is a sort of feeling more allied to the emotions than to anything else. . . . [R]eality means simply relation to our emotional and active life.*"[33] Emotion is defined at once as belief and as interpretation. To believe is to interpret an event as "real," that is, to make signs signify. Belief is indeed the "sense of reality." What we believe is real we interpret as real. Therein lies a fundamental tendency of consciousness. "*The primitive impulse is to affirm immediately the reality of all that is conceived. . . .* We would believe everything if we only could."[34]

When James states that belief is the "sense of reality," he signals, paradoxically enough, that the existence of things outside me does not depend on my belief. In other words, I believe that things exist independently of my belief that they exist. Thus to say, "I believe that things exist outside my perception of them," and to say, "things exist outside my perception of them," is to say the same thing, practically speaking.[35] The existence of an external world is indeed a postulate, but it is a postulate we cannot do without. Yes, there is an external world, objective, independent of us, which precedes the experience we have of it.[36] Things are there "before" us. This is one of our first beliefs. There is nothing arbitrary about it; it is the result not of a choice, but of an interpretation we find ourselves constrained to. There is something in the event that makes me perceive it as independent of my perception (but not such that it would be independently of my perception).

The events of pure experience are shocks, so to speak, and not something that we can make or represent. And such shocks constrain us to affirm the thing as external to our perception. Between the world and us, there is an incessant shock that forces us to believe in its exteriority by its brutality and unexpected character: "That reality is 'independent' means that there is something in every experience that escapes our arbitrary control. If it be a sensible experience it coerces our attention; if a sequence, we cannot invert it; if we compare two terms we can come to only one result. *There is a push, an urgency, within our very experience, against which we are on the whole powerless, and which drives us in a direction that is the destiny of our belief.*"[37]

Nonetheless, we should not assume that belief is born of a purely physical or physiological shock. Regarding reality as exterior to us does not mean that we must submit to its principle: on the contrary, we have to make reality, to put it into signs, because to believe is to interpret the shock as real. Such is the definition of perception in James, and more generally that of belief: interpreting as real, signifying as real. "That our perceptions mean *beings* . . . becomes an *interpretation* [my emphasis] so luminous of what happens to us that, once employed, it never gets forgotten."[38] In other words, the shock is for us at the same time a *sign*, a sign of exteriority. Events become real through an immediately violent interference.

It is only later, to the extent that shocks multiply and signs grow one on another, that a context is progressively formed, at the heart of which our beliefs come to be inscribed, and through which they are determined. A powerful determinism, tied at once to what the world forces us to think and to what our habits (imprinted in nervous circuits) also lead us to infer, spares us the shocks, which are deadened by the context greeting them. Signs thus become real by the simple fact that they are in tune with the ground of acquired habits and the present context accompanying them. The pure present of the shock trails off, to make room for the sense of temporal continuity. Believing no longer only means interpreting the shock but also means interpreting multiple shocks in accord with the ground of belief that is progressively constructed within us and that transforms our perceptions into preperceptions. Then, and only then, "real" applies less to the shock and more to the accord, so much so that it becomes easy to assume that the function of the knowing subject consists precisely in producing this accord, and to assume that knowledge is constituted by a subject. Thus the illusion may be born that accord comes first. Genesis then steps in too late, when everything is done.

It is easy to see what objections might be raised here. James rejects the necessity for recourse to an ego; and yet, do belief, emotion, interpretation, or whatever we call them, not always imply the underlying presence of an ego that believes, rises up, and interprets? Such a question inverses the order of priority: what is first are not interpretations, beliefs, not an "I believe" but an intensity, an emotion that traverses us and makes us believe. It is not a subject that produces interpretations but the inverse: the subject is made within interpretations; or more precisely, the subject is itself an interpretation, an interpretation of corporeal affections: "I am as confident as I am of anything that, in myself, the stream of thinking . . . is only a careless name for what, when scrutinized, reveals itself to consist chiefly of the stream of my breathing. The 'I think' which Kant said must be able to accompany all my objects, is the 'I breathe' which actually does accompany them."[39] Such provocative formulations may be seen as James's way of illustrating a psychophysiological postulate; but on a more fundamental level, they underscore that material may be interpreted as a respiratory flow or a mental flow. In either case, what comes first is the emotion that is inseparable from the bodily affection determining the interpretation.

James once again comes close to the Bergson of *Matter and Memory* when he evokes the "central image" of the body.[40] Indeed James writes,

> The world experienced (otherwise called the "field of consciousness") comes at all times with our body as its centre, centre of vision, centre of action, centre of interest. Where the body is is "here"; when the body acts is "now"; what the body touches is "this"; all other things are "there" and "then" and "that." These words of emphasized position imply a systematization of things with reference to a focus of action and interest which lies in the body. . . . The body is the storm centre, the origin of co-ordinates, the constant place of stress in all that experience-train. Everything circles round it, and is felt from its point of view. The word "I," then, is primarily a noun of position, just like "this" and "here."[41]

The initial "that" passes into a series of "here," "there," "now." A series of signs is created, radiating outward from the body. The first individuating factors are produced from these humble substitutes, which will lead to the construction of consciousness, but as if consciousness, in its turn, was only the integration of the repercussions of bodily affections. Personal experience corresponds to lines on a sort of map that is the projection of a focal point, the topographical relief of its dynamic relations with objects laid out panoramically around the body and its field of virtual action.

Because the body is always at the center of so-called subjective experiences, I interpret it as me. Nevertheless it cannot be said that the body is the me, in a sort of reversed Cartesianism; rather the body belongs to me, provided the me is nothing other than this act of ever-renewed appropriation, as outlined in the previous passages. For the invariable self, James substitutes the continuous variation of mineness. This means that the spreading out, or rather the filling in, of the field of consciousness varies from moment to moment. Sometimes consciousness contracts and diminishes the field of what it calls mine (in states of fatigue, for example); sometimes, on the contrary, it enlarges its horizon and expands into new connections (as our energy returns).[42] Mineness is a matter not of counting my possessions, but of something that I thought was within my power but that could suddenly become impossible because I am exhausted, or my body falls into deep asthenia. The consciousness thinks, but the body bounds what I may think, what is within my power to think. The focusing—or consciousness—is formed by the maps it draws up, the map of what its body can do. These first interpretations make way for a second interpretation superimposed on them. I interpret myself as a self on the basis of sampling a certain number of relations that are "neutral" in themselves—which is another way of saying there is no self. "Self" is a convention that designates an ensemble of mobile coordinates: it names a position.

Function and Convention (against Hylomorphism)

What we thus discover through the horizon of pure experience is that the material-event does not function as matter for forms or categories. We find that there are no forms, or rather that forms are not constitutive. What do we find "in their place"? Functions and nothing but functions. Material is matter for functions or creations. Far from being constitutive, forms are always derived from a function that produces them.[43] There are not formations of matter but series of materials. In addition, rather than general forms, we look for a subject-function, an object-function, a knowledge-function, a reality-function, and so forth. One of the passages in which James recapitulates his ideas speaks clearly to such a substitution:

> This "pen," for example, is, in the first instance, a bald *that*, a datum, fact, phenomenon, content, or whatever other neutral or ambiguous name you may prefer to apply. I called it . . . "pure experience." To

get classed either as a physical pen or as some one's percept of a pen, it must assume a *function*, and that can only happen in a more complicated world. . . . The pen, realized in this retrospective way as my percept, thus figures as a fact of "conscious" life. But it does so only so far as "appropriation" has occurred; and appropriation is *part of the content of a later experience* wholly additional to the originally "pure" pen. *That* pen, virtually both objective and subjective, is at its own moment actually and intrinsically neither.[44]

Form no longer defines anything. For the matter/form pair (tools of theoretical construction), radical empiricism substitutes a new relation, material/function (tools of practical construction). The first instance is a matter of legislating (subordinating the material of the datum to the legality of pure forms to determine their meaning). The second is a matter of creating (increasing reality through the production of interpretations through conventions of signs). In one case, the "critical," or phenomenological, method makes us into legislators (because the project is theoretical), and in the other case, the method makes us creators (because the project is practical).

All major concepts are thus destroyed as constitutive forms but are restituted as constitutive functions. For instance, when James asks in his famous essay "Does Consciousness Exist?" he replies in the negative yet adds: the notion of consciousness answers quite well to a function or an ensemble of functions destined for knowing.[45] In this sense, the real question is: What are the functions beneath a given pure form? In this first aspect, radical empiricism gives rise to a generalized functionalism. Again, the question is no longer a series of interrogations into the form or essence of what is in question: What is the subject? What is the object? What is knowledge? Instead we ask, For a given material, what are the possible and virtual functions? This is why a single event may be considered either subjective or objective, depending on the function that we bring into play.

Although the vast neutral horizon of pure experience possesses a genetic power, it is not to be confused in any way with what is original. The point of view that comes with it is not originary but naïve. Naïveté has nothing to do with any sort of credulity or ignorance, for if ignorance is a state that may be quickly overcome, naïveté is a state that may be covered over but not overcome. As a matter of fact, naïveté is merely what allows us to perceive the overcoming. From this point of view, Husserl was wrong to reject naïveté so quickly and to replace it with the Cartesian method of doubt, however much renewed. Both James and Peirce, in their particular manners, are opposed to the method of doubt, which remains too burdened with implicit assumptions. Doubt is always directed toward a fundamental certainty for which it serves as a precursor sign. The moment inevitably comes when doubt is turned back on itself to institute as a first principle a power of constitution already manifested by doubt in its ability to hold matters in suspension. The subject is posited in principle, but at the same time, it does not know that an entire world precedes it, which the subject has the illusion of producing for itself. The method of doubt does not permit us to see that the subject is also a construction. The plane of pure experience is the horizon on which all beliefs, all constructions, all interpretations are seen to arise. The "strangeness" of this point of view, at once purely immanent to experience and radically exterior to constitutive forms, makes everything appear to be convention.

If James continues to speak of "consciousness," of "object" and "subject," it is the result of convention. His discussion makes clear that, for him, the terms "I" and "ego" and "subject" refer to an entirely other effective reality: naming a position. Thus, rather than an invariable "I," a mobile consciousness must be put forward, which places and transplants its coordinates as a function of the new relations the body never ceases to establish within a skein of relations, which is also perpetually changing. A subject is, by convention, an ensemble of coordinates organized from the bundle of relations passing through the body.

We act *as if* that was consciousness, an objective reality, and so forth, for the sake of ease. We would have to put all these concepts in quotation marks, as Nietzsche does (and sometimes James) to underscore their conventional, interpretative, and functional nature. Everything becomes convention, including operative functions. That means that concepts are destroyed in their legislative capacity yet restored in their capacity as conventions. It is possible to consider any given material as subjective or objective, but this is a matter of convention, since material is actually neither the one nor the other. A form is only a symbolic function. Functionalism and conventionalism are combined and expressed in the same question: *What function* does a given material serve?

If all is convention (or interpretation), not all conventions have the same merit. Only functional conventions should be accepted as well founded. Consequently, a rigorous method must be established, which deals only with functions and provides the means to deal with them. Functions must be paid close attention, to determine which is the function of consciousness, of concepts, of action, of truth, and so forth. Pragmatism is such a method, which we may now presume to be more rigorous than the abusive simplifications to which it has usually been subjected, which treat it as a simple order of subjective appreciation and an arbitrary method of psychological validation.

TRUTH AND KNOWLEDGE

2

How to Create Truths?

Insofar as the pragmatic method consists of dealing with ideas, in terms of function not form, we need to ask not what the idea is, but what it does. The idea is considered no longer in light of *what is thought*, but in terms of *what it makes us think*. The traditional definitions of the idea as image, representation, or modification of the mind are incomplete, as they do not take into account its essential property: producing effects in our thinking and in our body. The idea acts; and whenever it acts, it makes us act. From the pragmatic point of view, an idea is thus inseparable from its consequences. It produces an effect on thinking, in the form of another idea becoming associated with it, a perception that individuates it, or an action that prolongs it. The idea is a process.

What then is the function of the idea? The idea has the particular property of directing our thought in a specific direction. Ideas are guides. "Not where it comes from but what it leads to is to decide."[1] The essential function of the idea is not to represent reality adequately or to establish correspondences between an image in the mind and an object in reality. James denies that ideas are copies of a preexisting physical or material reality. "To copy a reality is, indeed, one very important way of agreeing with it, but it is far from being essential. The essential thing is the process of being guided."[2] It is less a matter of representing realities than of establishing their coordinates. How, within the mental geography, do we go from one idea to another, from one reality to another? An idea is that through which a consciousness orients and directs the flow of thought traversing it. As James says, "By combining concepts with percepts, *we can draw maps of the distribution* of other percepts in distant space and time. . . . the conceptual map-making has enormous practical importance."[3] An idea imparts a direction. We are directed, mentally or physically, toward the aimed-for object through a series of intermediary signs and collateral experiences that lead us to it or into its vicinity. The previous discussion, wherein consciousness was tracing out its first references and establishing its maps by following the potentiality of its body, already attested to this function. Consciousness develops because it "follows" the ideas thanks to which it is led or directed.

Nonetheless, it is not possible to be guided or led unless the idea is effectively in agreement with the reality it aspires to travel through. In other words, there must be some guarantee that ideas are acquainted with this reality. Even though we take this reality to be constructed by interpretations, such interpretations must nonetheless guarantee for us the truth of what they put forth. This question becomes all the more crucial because, for James, resemblance no longer constitutes a decisive criterion for the relation of consciousness. What then assures us that beliefs and interpretations make for effective knowledge? Put another way, what definition of the truth is pragmatism able to propose? James's response is well known: "*The true is the name of whatever proves itself to be good in the way of belief, and good, too, for definite, assignable reasons.*"[4] Yet if belief and truth are thus identified, and if belief depends on the intensity of our emotions, do we not fall into relativism or subjectivism, as some of James's critics have been quick to point out? If an idea becomes real—or true—only as an object of belief, isn't knowledge given over to the arbitrariness of the belief itself? And so much so that we would quickly arrive at the absurdity Russell pointed out? "The statement that 'A exists' may be true in the pragmatic sense even if A does not exist," and, "It follows . . . that if A believes one thing and B believes the opposite, A and B may both be believing truly."[5] What criteria then are at our disposal for distinguishing between beliefs that are related to a real object and those that are thoroughly fanciful, such as hallucinations, errors, and illusions?

In pragmatic terms, the question may thus be formulated: What is the process through which truth is constructed? Here we return to definitions that have raised such polemic responses and misunderstanding: truth always comes to an idea from without, since the consequences to which truth leads determine it. As one of the best-known passages from James puts it, "The truth of an idea is not a stagnant property inherent in it. Truth *happens* to an idea. It *becomes* true, is *made* true by events."[6] Yet this only displaces the objections. James confronted no end of philosophical criticisms, which, for all their numbers, may be reduced to one major objection: James's pragmatism is reproached for making the truth of an idea depend on extrinsic conditions. On the one hand, truth is made dependent on its practical consequences (while these do not properly belong to the idea), and on the other hand, it is identified with a subjective feeling of satisfaction (while it, too, is a concomitant and nonconstitutive phenomenon, whence its departure from logical functions, for instance). In other words, James's pragmatism is subjectivism and relativism. Truth is nothing other than what a subject makes of it (consequences), nothing other than the feeling a subject experiences (satisfaction). Truth no longer possesses necessity or universality.

Each objection needs to be considered separately. Let's begin with satisfaction. We know that the idea is true when its consequences are satisfying for the one who is led to it. An idea is thus not true in itself. What makes possible its truth is the satisfaction obtained by its consequences: "Yet at each and every concrete moment, truth for each man is what that man 'troweth' at that moment with the maximum of satisfaction to himself. . . . [T]he true and the satisfactory do mean the same thing."[7] Satisfaction here is not any more relative or arbitrary than belief was previously. I may always say that I find it satisfactory to believe that a spirit apparition is real rather than a hallucination, or that the Loch Ness monster exists, or that Spinoza did not die of natural causes but at the hand of his doctor. James has always granted as much to his critics. What is forgotten in each of these examples is the domain from which they are taken: it is always a domain in which I am effectively free to choose a certain hypothesis over another.

In such a case, satisfaction acts, in effect, as a subjective criterion, varying in accordance with the motivations of each individual. We might then suppose that it is possible to find any belief whatsoever satisfactory, or, as Russell puts it, to affirm A even if A does not exist. In short, we find that satisfactions based on error may exist. But such an approach forgets that satisfaction results precisely from the relation between belief and truth.

For an idea to prove satisfactory, that is, true, it must be in agreement with contextual reality and with the background of logical habits the mind has accumulated. Satisfaction is consequently subject to *conditions* and is not at all arbitrary. It comes with the harmony felt between these two contexts. For the most part, the idea is true only because it stabilizes the link between the inventory of ideas accumulated in the course of our experience and the new reality presented to us.[8] We would not find satisfaction in ideas in contradiction with one of these two sets. "We must find a theory that will *work*; and that means something extremely difficult; for our theory must mediate between all previous truths and certain new experiences. . . . To 'work' means both these things; and the squeeze is so tight that there is little loose play for any hypothesis."[9]

Contrary to Russell's assumptions, we are not free to believe in anything whatsoever or to think whatever we like; and because satisfaction goes hand in hand with what we are constrained to believe, it is no longer possible to look at it in terms of arbitrary validation. There remains, however, the problem of illusions, which seems to confirm Russell's account. Doesn't being in a state of illusion affirm the existence of A when A does not exist? James might well reply: such an idea is true for the one who believes in it, even if it is an illusion, even if it is a hallucination (to maintain that ghosts exist and so forth), and false for the one who does not believe in it.

Illusions and hallucinations are not at all arbitrary (they are only possible when nothing in experience contradicts them); and often they are even prepared at length and in secret before appearing to the mind with an explosive intensity. And this is equally true of ghostly apparitions: an entire context is needed prior to their appearance, a reality propitious for them to appear without contradiction, for us really to believe in them. An idea must always have been prepared; it is never limited to a proposition of the type "A thinks that ghosts exist."

James's thesis does not imply the least relativism; it is a matter of saying not that "everything is relative" but that any truth is inseparable from the point of view stating it. Indeed a statement has *meaning* only under such conditions. Perspectivism is not relativist; it refers to a function of interpretation. As such, a statement should not be considered as a simple abstract proposition as Russell does. How can the truth-value of such propositions be evaluated independently of the meaning that they take on within a given context?

Insofar as an idea acts, it is not an isolated element (as the proposition is). It builds a go-between, a transitive reality inserted into a context—without which it is stripped of signification.[10] Truth is no longer the quality of an idea; it is, as James says, "a collective name for a process of verification," a series in becoming. Truth is never applied to the idea alone, but to its development; and this is because each moment of consciousness forms a field, part of which remains vague, uncertain, virtual. Truth comes about through its consequences, but the consequences may not be separated from the idea since they are its development. Rationalism, or what James calls "vicious abstractionism," in its impulse to eliminate all psychology, ignores that an idea is a part of the flow of consciousness. An idea wells up from the obscure indeterminate ground of consciousness to propel itself into a future that is equally indeterminate. Truth is a property inherent to the idea if and only if it is conceived of as a simple representation without movement—in an abstract manner. Abstractionism went so far astray because it wished to consider truth and, in a general way, the theory of consciousness assumed by it, without recourse to psychology. In fact, abstractionism implicitly provided a psychology, but because it did not clearly expound it, it met with failure. It is not possible to abstract the idea from consciousness to examine what validity it has in itself. On the contrary, the idea has to be immersed in consciousness to determine what makes us believe in its truth.

By considering the extent to which pragmatism reinvigorates the conception of truth, we may better understand why it has evoked so much misunderstanding. The philosophical tradition—principally rationalism—thinks of truth as based on a preexisting model to which the idea must be referred. This is why it does nothing but discover a truth preexisting in reality in-itself (physical or metaphysical). Newton's laws indeed discovered a structure that preexisted their discovery. For all eternity, bodies are subjected to gravitational force. Under such conditions, it goes without saying that the truth of Newtonian laws would not depend on the physicist's feeling of satisfaction, apart from reducing scientific laws to their psychological concomitants. How could we maintain in such an instance that the idea is true by virtue of satisfying effects? Should we not say, on the contrary, that effects are only satisfying because the idea is first of all true? If I say that the Big Dipper is composed of seven stars, doesn't the truth always come of the fact that there have always been exactly these seven stars? In this way, truth is defined as a relationship of correspondence with an invariable reality in-itself. It reaches the point where verifying an idea does not demand looking ahead to the consequences toward which it orients us but consists of looking back at the principle on which it depends. Thus, in what James generically calls "rationalism," the relation of truth is thought on the model of eternal truths. Rationalists examine the idea not as action but only as retroaction.

The originality of pragmatism lies in considering the truth based not on eternal ideas but on new ideas. All our ideas are initially experimental. Affirming the existence of an external world is an experimental hypothesis: I go beyond the data of initial sensations to put forth the hypothesis that there must exist an "objective" reality independent of my perception of it. To say that pragmatism rejects the model of eternal truths also means that it presents a vast and powerful critique of representation—for three fundamental reasons. Ideas are not reproductions or representations because first they are actions, and then they are transitions, and finally and especially they are creations. It is easy then to understand why resemblance cannot be the general model of truth, unless we say that resemblance is itself created, as an artist creates resemblance in a portrait. And in the same way that "producing resemblance" is not the only goal of the artist, resemblance in philosophy, too, is but a means of being led, guided, and even forced toward other realities.

Take again the example of the Big Dipper. A specific constellation being discovered and given a name is apparently just a matter of discovering something that has existed forever. But, James asks, why project a recent thought into an eternal past? Were there exactly seven stars, and did they explicitly resemble a dipper before thought made such a distinction? They were only what we came to call them, virtually; thought explicated them and rendered them real, even if the stars themselves dictated the result. Such a thought is thus irreducibly novel; it copies nothing that preexists, although it is in agreement with what preexists, amplifying it, describing it and connecting it with a dipper, constructing it.[11]

The second objection addressed to James is that truth can depend on practical consequences only when they belong intrinsically to the idea. Because the word truth does not have a verb that speaks to its process,

James reserves the verb "verify" for such a purpose. The idea or concept becomes true when it is verified. The verb "verify" should not mislead us. It is not a retroactive process of confirmation; *verification is the act of creating the idea.* Truth is a process. Why are ideas inseparable from a process of verification? Precisely because they are at once beliefs and creations. As beliefs, they cannot be certain of what they posit; as creations, they do not know in advance what they will produce. This is why we cannot know if an idea is true before having tested its validity: "Truth *happens* to an idea. It *becomes* true, is *made* true by events. Its verity *is* in fact an event, a process: the process namely of its verifying itself, its veri-*fication*. Its validity is the process of its valid-*ation*."[12] Verifying consists of exploring the context associated with the orientation given by the idea, thus individualizing and concretizing the idea. Our new ideas are hypotheses that must be tested through their consequences. Consequences thus are truly, rightfully inseparable from the process of verification. Thus verifying does not consist of exposing a truth initially contained in the idea but entails creating that very truth. Resemblance obviously does not allow us to determine the truth of a new idea since by definition truth does not resemble anything.

The idea makes for acting, thinking, but in a specific direction. The idea orients us toward its practical verification, toward what James calls "practical consequences." It is important to clear up a common misunderstanding in this respect. Because James says that true ideas "pay" and bring a "return," it might be assumed that the idea is true to the extent that it serves action, understood as technical or utilitarian activity, or allows for financial or commercial gain. In short, practice is associated with "convenience" or "efficiency," as if practice did not also apply to theory. It is not that a theory must become practice, but rather theory is a practice of invention and creation. The pragmatic rule applies equally to thought insofar as it is distinct from action.[13] "Practical" is thus opposed not to "theoretical," but to the vague or abstract. "When we spoke of the meaning of ideas consisting in their 'practical' consequences . . . we were almost unanimously held to mean *opposed* to theoretical or genuinely cognitive. . . . Again, by the practical one often means the distinctively concrete, the individual, particular, and effective, as opposed to the abstract, general, and inert. To speak for myself, whenever I have emphasized the practical nature of truth, this is mainly what has been in my mind."[14]

What allows rationalism to declare that the idea is true in itself? It looks at truth only in terms of already constituted ideas, already verified beliefs, which is to say habits, for the most part. In effect, only when the idea *returns* in a habit is it possible to say that it was *already* true in itself. Rationalism steps in after the fact. And, as always, there is no choice but to bring judgment to bear retroactively, to say that the idea was already intrinsically true, for us to discover its preexistence through its consequences. The world was there before we discovered its existence. What is true was always true. Russell's objection only makes sense through such a conflation. The rationalist order is not valid precisely because rationalism does not distinguish between new ideas and habit-ideas, between verification and verifiability. The first instance I anticipate; the second I predict.[15] Prediction is nothing but anticipation turned into habit, and they are not different in nature, nor is there difference in nature between essential truths and existential truths, or between conjecture and science. The error of rationalism is to reverse the real order, to bring verifiability into play before verification.

To James, the term "verifiability" has two distinct meanings. In the first sense, verifiability is knowledge bought on credit as opposed to knowledge with the cash value of verification. Verifiability is defined as *possible* verification: we dispense with verification because it is not necessary when the effects of the idea are already known—which allows rationalists to declare that truth is inherent in the idea, that it comes prior to its verification. When it is a matter of habit-ideas or ideas derived from habits, of course we know the idea is true before applying it, since we have already experienced its effects. A concept then is the idea of the thing plus what we expect from it.

In the second sense, however, verifiability is a potential or *virtual* verification. "*Indirectly or only potentially verifying processes may thus be true as well as full verification-processes.*"[16] For each idea, we have an obscure feeling, on the edges of consciousness, that verifies the idea by rapid anticipatory visions, to the point where the virtual and actual are scarcely distinguishable.[17] An abbreviated sort of verification is at work, even though an effective or determinate verification has never come into play. Something indeterminate is hovering over. I vaguely feel a form in the pockets of my vest; it must be my keys. We feel affinities, the "agreement" between our idea and reality, at a glance, through an intuitive testing of the context. "Now the immensely greater part of all our knowing never gets beyond this virtual stage. . . . We live, as it were, upon the front edge of an advancing wave-crest, and our sense of a determinate direction in falling forward is all we cover of the future of our path."[18] We need not verify because the weight of the context, dimly felt, near or distant, gives sufficient sign to provoke our belief. Verifiability here merges with a feeling of faith. We no longer need to complete our verifications, any more than our perceptions need every detail of the perceptual field, or any more than our thoughts need to actualize all at once everything impinging in on them from the edges. Signs suffice. They act, most of the time, as condensed versions of verification, or, to use James's turns of phrase, shortcuts and abridgements.

Strictly speaking, pragmatism proposes not so much a new definition of truth as a method of experimentation, a method for constructing new truths. To experiment is to consider theory as a creative practice. This is why truth is a matter not of knowing what is true but of knowing how the true is made. And this question is inseparable from another: What does the true make? A true idea, in the pragmatic sense, is an idea that changes something in the mind of the person thinking, in a satisfactory manner. The true idea is not only what we believe, what we do, or what we think; it is what makes us believe, makes us act, or makes us think. At the same time, then, pragmatism is a method for evaluating the truth. We no longer judge an idea, a doctrine, or a statement as a function of their truth; on the contrary, the truth of an idea, a doctrine, or a statement is a function of its consequences for thought, action, or belief. In this respect, pragmatism is an instrumentalism. It might be said, as pragmatism's detractors do, that the notion of truth as such is eliminated. In effect, truth is now evaluated as the function of a value that surpasses it in epistemological value—what holds our interest. What good is a truth without interest, that is, a truth that does not make us act, believe, or think? This is the primary reason that the notion of resemblance gradually ceases to constitute a decisive criterion. "Why may not thought's mission be to increase and elevate, rather than simply to imitate and reduplicate, existence?"[19] It is legitimate to ask wherein lies the interest of testing the value of the truth of such propositions as "Caesar is dead" or "the cat is on the mat." What in them makes us think or act? More generally, it becomes necessary at a certain point to judge philosophies by what they make us believe, think, or do (which are one and the same). We do not create or act for the truth. It only turns out that our ideas are true. We act and think to increase and elevate what exists.

If truth is indeed action, transition, creation (rather than representation, conclusion, imitation), it is to the extent that "full truth [is] the truth that energizes and does battle."[20] We have to reach a point where we extricate ourselves from the ground of ancestral habits that we have contracted (and that burden us with the full weight of the past)—what James calls common sense—which affect us to the point where we sometimes succumb to what James calls "old fogyism," a sort of premature solidification of thought. This is what makes creation so difficult. We have to loosen the tight weave of solid habits to introduce new connections into it, to sew new pieces onto it that will extend it and bring about new ramifications. This is what we now need to examine, because we do not yet have the logic allowing us to think the new.

Lines and Pieces

What James discovers through pure experience, what he raises to the level of a primary condition, are *relations*. Ultimately, radical empiricism appears as a theory of relations, free of substance, of all inherent properties, and of all essential attributions; material must be liberated from the forms on which it has been made to depend. In keeping with the empiricist tradition, relations are exterior to their terms.[21] Only thus is immanence possible: if relations are made to depend on a subject or a substance, immanence is then lost, and the very nature of the relation as well; it becomes static, and the model of eternal truths once again comes to constitute the horizon on the basis of which relations are thought. The danger lies in interrupting movement or enclosing it within concepts.[22] So keen is this danger that a type of knowledge is required that does not imprison the movement of relations within preexisting forms, or terms in preexisting relations. We must pursue continuity, the great continuous plane of pure experience, and proceed through the intertwining of relations.

But what is to be done when there is no longer subject or object, when knowledge no longer takes recourse to such coordinates, when knowledge is entrusted to the movement of the knowledge function? This is the problem that pluralism poses in relation to pure experience. In effect, to be pluralist consists of allowing relations to be laid out in all directions. The multiple is right out in the open, so to speak. But what concepts will enable us to think on this pluralist field without falling back on unity? The problem is all the more difficult in that plurality cannot be thought in its pure state.[23] Such a world would truly be chaos, with each and every one of its parts subjected to radical dispersion. Unities (or totalities) are therefore necessary. Thus, through such questions about continuity and plurality, the following question arises: How is knowledge to proceed effectively once our concepts work through discontinuous and unifying slices?

What is offered to us is a distribution of events. The Whole forms a collection, nothing more than a plurality of terms, anarchic disparate singularities. This is the point of departure for most philosophies, from classical empiricism to absolutist monism. They put emphasis on disjunctions, in the form of either atomist dispersion or phenomenal appearances. It is clear why absolutists would proceed thus. James cites a disciple of Hegelian philosophy, Thomas Hill Green, who remarks, "Yes! *Terms* may indeed be possibly sensational in origin; but *relations*, what are they but pure acts of the intellect coming upon the sensations from above, and of a higher nature?"[24] Yet his description of the datum is already too constructed: How does he not see that relations are perceived at the same time as the terms they link? To perceive a set of terms as disparate only means that we perceive disjunctive relations. We do not perceive two terms separately, only to bring the two together subsequently. To counter absolutism, we must say that we perceive them directly as different. There is a shock, a sensation of difference, the shock of thunder breaking the silence. I do not perceive n and then m to infer their difference afterward. The series given is n, then m being different from n.[25]

The principle of radical empiricism lies in rejecting any element we do not directly experience; but it is imperative not to exclude the realities of which experience is made: we experience disjunctions, but contrary to empiricism in this instance, we may equally well experience connections.[26] The objection may arise that connections can only be made if the terms are first perceived as disjunctive. If not, what would there be to connect? There is, however, a shock of likeness just as there is a shock of difference. To return to the previous example, we might say that the second thunderclap is perceived directly as being like the first. Once again, we do not perceive n, then m, and then n being like m. Likeness is perceived at the same time as the second term. We are thus in the presence of a set of multiplicities shot through with relations that are sometimes disjunctive and sometimes connective in accordance with the series of shocks we experience.

It is easier to understand the basis for the objections to empiricism if we hear the term "continuity" behind the term "conjunction." When James says that there is an experience of connections, he means that we feel continuities, that continuities are givens. Put another way, where empiricism sees only juxtapositions of psychic atoms, James finds copenetrations, continuous flows. The stream of consciousness constitutes precisely a continuum within which disjunctions appear discontinuous, if the analysis is pushed too far. The relation of difference, however, cannot serve as a sign of discontinuity of any sort, since the relation is incorporated into the very terms it separates. The "sensation of difference" is not only given "in the brief instant of transition"; it is fairly incorporated into the second term that feels "different from the first" for as long as it lasts. The relation of difference is a mixture of continuity and discontinuity. As Jean André Wahl says, "What is most contrary to analysis is less the continuous in itself than the apparent mixture of continuous and discontinuous found in rhythm, or a volume, or a person."[27]

In this respect, James distinguishes three large continuums: consciousness, time, and space. We have already seen that time is not a discontinuous reality, constituted of instants, but a continuous flow in which past, present, and future intermingle. The present does not constitute a separable unity but is a relative "block" of duration, what James calls the "specious present." Likewise, space assures continuity between the diverse individual flows of consciousness that would otherwise be radically separated. In effect, although we cannot be sure if we are perceiving the same object, I can nonetheless seize the very perspective by which someone else perceives it.[28] Streams of consciousness are separated absolutely, as monads are. "I can only define 'continuous' as that which is without breach, crack, or division. I have already said that the breach from one mind to another is perhaps the greatest breach in nature."[29] There is an inalienable and irreducibly private ground to which no one may have access except the one who directly experiences it.[30]

If we are nonetheless in the same world, it is partly because of the existence of spatial continuity. We occupy the same space.[31] I may reconcile my space with that of another through the intermediary of like objects. We may then speak of minds being coterminous, of the coterminousness of minds in the sense that perceptions terminate on the same object. For instance, someone else may feel her body to be where I perceive it to be. Between me and someone else is a community of space and not a simple juxtaposition, because our spaces penetrate each other through the intermediary of objects that serve as points of intersection or allow for partial recovery. In this sense, space is indeed constructed through connections. Distance is an edge-to-edge, piece-by-piece construction, a patchwork operation. We no longer proceed through associations between atoms but through connecting and stringing together. She acts in my space; I act in hers. Space cannot be defined as a general form that an empirical sensibility then happens to fill, any more than consciousness or time can be; on the contrary, space is presented as a continuous multiplicity with multiple connections. Once again, however, these three large continuities also present appearances of discontinuity, with their specific rhythms. Consciousness is a flow, yet each pulsation that courses through it, each field that passes, is "shut in its own skin, windowless, ignorant of what the other feelings are and mean."[32] Likewise, the flow of time presents itself as an agent of separation characterized by irreversibility. Ultimately, if space is what can reunite consciousnesses, it is also what separates them. Continuity and discontinuity follow their respective thread of connections or disjunctions. There is no reality within which the two types of relation cannot be detected.

This is why James submits that the world is one and at the same time not one, because relations are sometimes connective, sometimes disjunctive, according to the shocks received and the series covered. It is impossible to know in advance since relations are not interior to their terms. James frequently makes such an affirmation: there is continuity everywhere, but all is not continuous in fact, because of disjunctions. Lines consist of series of intermediaries that sometimes operate as conductors, and sometimes do not. "Without being one throughout, such a universe is continuous. Its members interdigitate with their next neighbors in manifold directions, and there are no clean cuts between them anywhere."[33] Discontinuity always appears against the ground of continuity. The series that compose unities are prolonged in one another and, in this way, maintain the cohesiveness of the world. It is thus impossible to say whether we are dealing with a universe (absolute unity) or with a multiverse (absolute multiplicity), which is how we arrive at a pluriverse.[34]

This is precisely why James never let up in his battle against the monism of the One and All of absolutists and Hegelians. Surely no other philosophy is as consistently and explicitly turned against the idea of the All or the One, a relentless war machine that is applied at every level: psychological, metaphysical, logical, ethical.[35] Monists do indeed take the plurality of relations as a point of departure; and they no longer think of them as internal to substances, as does the classical movement of inclusion, which integrates mode into attribute, and attribute into substance; Hegelians introduce a properly dialectic movement into the concept, but ultimately only to better include plurality within the infinite interiority of Absolute Spirit. Thus the unity of the world forms a vast closed system: "The true must be essentially the self-reflecting self-contained recurrent, that which secures itself by including its own other and negating it; that makes a spherical system with no loose ends hanging out for foreignness to get a hold upon; that is forever rounded-in and closed, not strung along rectilinearly and open at its ends."[36] Although Hegelians actually begin with pluralism, such pluralism necessarily gives way to monism through implication.

Observations show that the world abides; despite incessant change, James says, it possesses relative stability. But for all that, it does not form a closed system. It owes its cohesion to an ensemble of *lines* that bind the universe.

> Lines of *influence* can be traced by which they hang together. Following any such line you pass from one thing to another till you may have covered a good part of the universe's extent. Gravity and heat-conduction are such all-uniting influences, so far as the physical world goes. Electric, luminous and chemical influences follow similar lines of influence. But opaque and inert bodies interrupt the continuity here, so that you have to step round them, or change your mode of progress if you wish to get farther on that day. Practically, you have then lost your universe's unity, *so far as it was constituted by those first lines of influence.*[37]

Following a *first dimension*, reality is formed of crisscrossed lines. An incalculable number of networks exist, superposed on one another, forming a vast reticular ensemble.[38] The world is a gigantic network. According to James's example, nature functions exactly like a postal network on which a telephone network is superposed, partially overlapping with it while nonetheless establishing specific connections, including new unities. Likewise the line of our auditory perceptions is naturally superposed on that of our visual perceptions, and the line of our concepts is superposed on these two lines, and so forth. Again likewise, we can constitute networks of knowledge.

> There are innumerable kinds of connexion that special things have with other special things; and the *ensemble* of any one of these connexions forms one sort of *system* by which things are conjoined. Thus men are conjoined in a vast network of *acquaintanceship*. Brown knows Jones, Jones knows Robinson, etc.; and *by choosing your farther intermediaries rightly* you may carry a message from Jones to the Empress of China, or the Chief of the African Pigmies, or to anyone

else in the inhabited world. But you are stopped short, as by a non-conductor, when you choose one man wrong in this experiment.[39]

Instead of establishing the cohesiveness of the world on the fusion of relations within an absolute, James invokes cohesiveness through a plurality of linear connections. When we ask how lines are made, a *second dimension* appears, for these lines are so many unities or systems. Only, instead of a grand unified system like that of the Hegelian dialectic, there are systems everywhere. These are indeed so many "little worlds."[40] Each of them presents a degree of unity as a function of its connections.

> Thus the lowest grade of universe would be a world of mere withness, of which the parts were only strung together by the conjunction "and." Such a universe is even now the collection of our several inner lives. . . . But add our sensations and bodily actions, and the union mounts to a much higher grade. Our *audita et visa* and our acts fall into those receptacles of time and space in which each event finds its date and place.[41]

There are indeed wholes and unities, but these are strictly immanent to multiplicities. It is such *unities of consistency* that ensure the cohesion and adhesion of the parts among themselves. Consistency is, in effect, that by which things hold together.[42] It may be said, for instance, that light is held together by eyes and by the photosynthesis of plants; conversely, plants are held together by light. There is unity in this respect, and that is all. All transcendence is thus rejected since the parts are no longer unified by a superior rationality—an exterior point of view; they hold each other together. Each thing that we attempt to pry loose bears with it a halo of connections, its region. "If you tear out one, its roots bring out more with them. . . . [W]hatever is real is telescoped and diffused into other reals."[43] Following the example of Gabriel Tarde, so many inventions, each of which may be foreign to the other—such as the invention of the train car (already complex in itself), of iron, of steam power, of the piston, and of rails—are nonetheless brought into solidarity within the invention of the locomotive that imparts consistency to them.[44] We would not say that such inventions are implied within one another—as Gottfried Wilhelm Leibniz would say that rape is included "within" the individual notion of Lucretia—rather, they are the ones *with* the others in a relationship of coalescence.[45] In the same way, relations would not be said to be *in* consciousness; they are *with* consciousness and impart consistency to it (thanks to the emotional intensity of the body). Consistency will become greater as the number of connections established by consciousness becomes larger.

Parts no longer give up their individuality within collective totalities; it is no longer a matter of fusion but is an ensemble of partial and relative conjunctions. It might be objected that such unities are incomplete, unfinished, and yet this is only true if unity is conceived of as rightfully superior to multiplicity.[46] We might here evoke, as does one commentator on James, an archipelago construction: "Without disrespect, we might compare the final unity in the philosophical thought of James to the geological unity of those ocean atolls first composed of isolated madrepores."[47] Such unities are bridges that tie together unities as so many islands. But they are also *fragments*, bits without borders or limits, without final unity, indefinitely open to construction and prolongation, in which each unity is tied to another by the line of its contours, in the manner in which one speaks of a fragment or a bit of cloth—to the point where, once again, the world appears as a vast patchwork. It is in this sense that James speaks of "mosaic philosophy."[48] The flow of the world is a stream of fragments, heterogeneous in their patterns, homogeneous in their stuff.

Line and fragment, *network* and *patchwork*, are the two great axes of construction of the world. The world is crosshatched with a skein of lines so entangled that they "let no individual elementary part of the universe escape" and yet at the same time do not close the universe on itself.[49] The universe is constituted of vast networks, sometimes conductive, sometimes nonconductive, which partially overlap and are prolonged in all directions, like so many means of transportation. Unities are incessantly broken up by disjunctive processes in accord with points of growth and bifurcation of the universe. This is why they can never be global or totalizing. The universe is a system of perpetual restarting: conjunctive lines integrate certain disjunctive processes but not without re-creating other disjunctions that escape them, and so on, in an unlimited manner, as if conjunctions were in pursuit of disjunctions. The world thus appears in an essentially discontinuous form, even if it is held together by continuities. In effect, with each new situation, the whole set of relations finds itself redistributed without any means of totalizing or unifying them. James's thought is akin to a John Dos Passos novel, describing the superpositions of connections, of the railway, maritime, and aerial networks, while mixing them with human biographies and bits of news reports, into the great synchronic novel of simultaneous and superposable itineraries. As James says, "We ourselves are constantly adding to the connexions of things, organizing labor-unions, establishing postal, consular, mercantile, railroad, telegraph, colonial, and other systems that bind us and things together in ever wider reticulations. . . . From the point of view of these partial systems, the world hangs together from next to next in a variety of ways."[50] It is indeed a matter of considering the world at once as a vast cloth pieced together bit by bit, and as a system of networks: patchwork and network.

Ambulatory Knowledge

To think is to be led by our ideas. We are led; we follow. Knowledge is a whole set of routes, conductions, prolongations, and connections rather than an act of transcending. Although to prolong and to anticipate effectively constitute acts of transcending, James rarely uses such a term because for him it means a leap into transcendence. That is the procedure of philosophies that begin with the subject or with consciousness. A leap is then always required to attain the object. And such a leap always consists of positing a condition exterior to the relation, to make it possible: a transcendental subject, an absolute mind. From the point of view of radical empiricism, the problem remains the same from classical metaphysics to transcendental philosophy and then absolutist philosophy:

> Throughout the history of philosophy the subject and its object have been treated as absolutely discontinuous entities; and thereupon the presence of the latter to the former, or the "apprehension" by the former of the latter, has assumed a paradoxical character which all sorts of theories had to be invented to overcome. Representative theories put a mental "representation," "image," or "content" into the gap, as a sort of intermediary. . . . Transcendentalist theories left it impossible to traverse by finite knowers, and brought an absolute in to perform the saltatory act.[51]

Certainly, the condition is no more exterior to knowledge than is the relation. It is no longer necessary to pass through God to guarantee or preestablish our relation to objects. Conditions may be brought down into the subject. A degree of immanence is indeed recovered in this way; but the passage through the transcendental remains. The problem is not resolved by Kant's successors, since their leap is accomplished in the Absolute:

relations are interior to an infinitely comprehensive Spirit. Everything begins with a dualism that they then endeavor to transcend, to surmount right away. And it is through such procedures that the leap comes to be performed. Building on this rather nice distinction, James calls this type of knowledge "saltatory." It relies on the principle whereby two terms are absolutely independent, and thus, to link them, a leap must be performed that will relate the one to the other within a common superior form. The leap consists of filling a ditch that we have created ourselves.

But isn't the act of belief saltatory for James? Is to believe not precisely to make the leap of transcendence? To the extent that belief interprets shocks, it is not a leap but a construction. It builds a footbridge to cross to the other bank. Intermediary terms are used to go from one term to another. Yet the terms of the series remain homogeneous, just as bits of space are linked to cover a distance. That relations are continuous does not mean that they are interior to the terms; rather, it means that they are homogeneous with them. The series thus constructed form bridges: "The idea however doesn't immediately leap the gulf, it only works from next to next so as to bridge it, fully or approximately."[52]

So it is that the existence of an object is not affirmed without passing through the context that accompanies it. And just as there is no substantial or formal unity to the subject, so there cannot be a form-object, except by convention. The object is not only defined as a group of heterogeneous qualities in the manner of classical empiricism; it extends a good deal beyond this relative unity. The object itself is also a complex of relations that may be prolonged. It is inseparable from its relations, although it does not imply them. As James says, it is impossible to extract an object without bringing some of its roots along with it. Thus the context, even in the virtual state, serves as an intermediary for us, not only to be led to the object, but also to posit the reality of it.[53] Once again, to interpret or to believe are not to make a leap but to go through series.

This is why James invokes a new type of knowledge that is not saltatory but ambulatory. Quite literally we roam through the intermediary series that lead us to provisional terms.

> My thesis is that the knowing here is *made* by the ambulation through the intervening experiences.... Those intermediaries determine what particular knowing function it exerts. The terminus they guide us to tells us what object it "means," the results they enrich us with

"verify" or "refute" it. Intervening experiences are thus as indispensable foundations for a concrete relation of cognition as intervening space is for a relation of distance. Cognition, whenever we take it concretely, means determinate "ambulation," through intermediaries, from a *terminus a quo* to, or towards, a *terminus ad quem*.[54]

It is literally a matter of building a bridge of actual or possible intermediaries.

To fill in the intervals does not mean that a preexisting form is to be replaced by empirical matter; it means that material must be organized in functional series. Knowledge, too, must construct lines. Such a constructivism is characteristic of radical empiricism, inseparable from the continuist hypothesis of pure experience.[55] "In the case of the epistemological chasm the first reasonable step is to remember that the chasm was filled with *some* empirical material, whether ideational or sensational, which performed *some* bridging function and saved us from the mortal leap."[56] Upon abstracting intermediaries, we end up with only two terms facing each other, finding ourselves obliged to take a leap. Or else, instead of building a bridge of empirical or ideal materials, we make a leap that is at once immobile and formal over an empty space. "For we first empty idea, object and intermediaries of all their particularities, in order to retain only a general scheme, and then we consider the latter only in its function of giving a result, and not in its character of being a process. . . . *In other words, the intermediaries which in their concrete particularity form a bridge, evaporate ideally into an empty interval to cross*, and then, the relation of the end-terms having become saltatory, the whole hocuspocus of *erkenntnistheorie* begins, and goes on unrestrained by further concrete considerations."[57] At the same token, we posit these forms as the foundation of any relation. As with the notion of truth, we posit them as anterior and essential because they act as principles. The leap has been made, once and for all: in its movement, it has seized on the principle whereby it posits a relation between the two terms that it has transcended.

In contrast, the empiricist is constrained to an incessant building of bridges, in every direction. The notions of intermediary and term must not fool us. Any term is at once relative and provisional; as such, it may of course enter into another series as an intermediary. *By convention we call the point of departure for a series "subject" and the point of arrival "object."* But they could equally well be called stemming from and heading for. The complete sequence (or what James calls a partial confluence) linking them is an act of knowledge. It is now clearer why knowledge is itself a continuous process and cannot come to an end: it is literally a flow, in the same way that there is a stream of consciousness. "... experience itself, taken at large, can grow by its edges. That one moment of it proliferates into the next by transitions which, whether conjunctive or disjunctive, continue the experiential tissue, cannot, I contend, be denied. Life is in the transitions as much as in the terms connected . . ."[58]

What may push us to believe that a leap must be made between subject and object is the way in which intermediaries become contracted, become abbreviated in habit, and then only take the form of a virtual border, taken in with a quick glance. The concept is in effect a conglomerate of virtual perceptions. We seem to leap from one object to another object, which actually exists; we seem to make associations in a discontinuous manner. But taking things in with a glance is not the same thing as leaping. *Relying on "virtualized" intermediaries is radically different from eliminating intervals.* Concepts are shortcuts, abbreviations, substitutes for intermediary series.[59] The problem is always the same: we bring in geneses after the fact, when everything is already constituted, and only what appear to be leaps are visible, and thus we do not take into account the intermediaries that have been abbreviated.[60]

Concepts are bits of condensed experience. They consolidate perceptions, and by incorporating them into the mass of anterior acquisitions, they form units of consistency. As in Bergson, perceptions and concepts are prehensions: they hold together the terms of some multiplicity or another; this is indeed what allows them to serve as maps.[61] Initial consistency is reinforced by a more extended consolidation in a manner rather like the one Chrysippus uses to describe knowledge, a hand gradually closing into a fist as knowledge becomes more consistent, solidified by the system of nature.[62] Such a definition of the concept harkens back to a physics of the mind, and to the act (or function) of holding, seizing. It is clear why James can interchangeably use verbs such as to consolidate, to consist, or to cohere, which are synonyms in English. To be coherent and to be consistent are one and the same thing: these are acts of consolidation. Coherence is what effectively makes consistency: the incorporation of our perceptions into the background of conceptual habits consolidates the whole and forms systems.[63] We are a "mystery of condensation."[64]

For James, knowledge is thus made step by step, bit by bit, without the bits converging on a final unity; knowledge creates its lines by making connections between diverse bits of experiences. It, too, creates its networks and patchworks. It may be thought that pragmatism extols American capitalism, not through the promotion of commercial and financial values in this instance, but through the description of great networks, indefinitely constructible ensembles with multiple linkages, which anticipates the massive development of communications networks in the twentieth century.

Yet if the philosopher is indeed one who roams ceaselessly among these vast networks, she seems to us closer to an itinerant traveler than to a businessperson. In effect, James's philosophy seems turned toward a social order less triumphant than that of the business milieu—that of hobos.[65] Hobos made for an immense dispersed flow of migrant workers moving across the United States, from Chicago all the way to the West Coast, looking for worksites and seasonal jobs and forming temporary local societies, "Hobohemia."[66] They are radically different from pioneers in the sense that they are inseparable from the movements of the American capitalist economy, with its alternating booms and sharp downturns, with its use of massive layoffs in combination with rapid rotation of the workforce. These rapid rhythms contribute to job instability and forced mobility, to "worker nomadism."[67]

Hobos are not sedentary workers and thus are not amenable to the remote control of labor unions. They fall in between, so to speak, between two "frontiers," that of first pioneer communities (who reached the Pacific around 1850) and that of industrialization (which completed its expansion around 1920). "The true hobo was the in-between worker, willing to go anywhere to take a job and equally willing to move on later. His in-between role related to the two frontiers. He came on the scene after the trail blazer, and he went off the scene as the second frontier was closing."[68] Hobos in effect went from one end of the country to another in an ambulatory manner, drawing on the vast network of connections to go in all directions, much as James describes the process of knowledge. They travel a stretch of route, stopping temporarily or moving on, following the paths of materials. How is it still possible to think of James's pragmatism as a philosophy for businessmen?

Needless to say, James's philosophy is not foremost a philosophy of knowledge. As we have seen, the idea is not a representation but that which spurs acting in a determined direction. Evidently, epistemology is thus inseparable from the practice in which it engages us. To know something is to know how to act on a reality based on an idea. The mistake of rationalist and absolutist philosophers comes precisely in enclosing knowledge on itself without prolonging it in a practice. In this way, they arrive at ideas that are only thought, at abstract representations, and at theoretical completion. In this way, they enclose relations in theoretical totalities for reflection, contemplation, or infinite speculation. Pragmatism, however, is a method for what is in the making, not for what is already made or for what should be made; it is in this respect antitheoretical. The theoretical viewpoint assumes, in effect, that knowledge has an end in itself, in a lawfully completed science, an object of contemplation, or a possession of wisdom. The practical viewpoint assumes that knowledge is de jure incomplete; that it is determined by exterior ends. And this is what James never stops doing, freeing us from such a theoretical closure: freeing material from its forms, freeing relations from inherence, freeing events from attribution, freeing truth from resemblance, freeing movement from immutability, freeing the ambulatory from the foundation, freeing multiplicities from unity, freeing the idea from representation; in brief, radical empiricism and pragmatism free philosophy from theoretical finality to render it copresent with its creative practice.

Once again, theory and practice do not designate two distinct activities such that the one would be exercised in the speculative, scientific domain, while the other would be exercised in the technical, utilitarian domain; they designate two points of view: the theoretical always comes in after the fact, after action, to think it (retrospectively); the practical comes with or at the same time as action for the action to happen (prospectively). For pragmatism, then, knowledge, or theory more generally, only guides or orients our activity; it does not constitute it. The problem lies in determining the conditions of practical activity. The problem might be formulated in the following manner: What makes us act? Or more precisely, What does an idea need for it to make us act? This is the ultimate question of pragmatism. It encourages inquiry into the problem of belief (psychological perspective), the problem of the idea (epistemological perspective), and the problem of finality (practical perspective).

We claim that the idea makes us act. And yet we do not think, we do not act, we do not know things simply because we can. We do not think a thought just to think it; we think it to think another. We thus think in order to act. There is always a moment, which can be prolonged indefinitely, in which we must venture into the indeterminate, without knowing for sure where connections will lead us. How does it happen that knowledge is constructed by series, and action brings about other actions, in an unbroken chain? What makes us pass from the idea to action, or from one idea to another? Rationality or coherence (when we find it) does not suffice to explain this passage. Something else is needed. What happens in the in-between such that we may constitute these sorts of series? We are asking an at once simple and odd question. Not "why do we act?" (which would lead us back to searching for the general reason for a first action), but "why do actions unfurl into actions?" (we seek, then, the reason for a chain of actions, a series). We thus seek *the reason of series.*

FAITH AND PRAGMATIC COMMUNITY

3

Having Faith

When he defines belief, James closely follows Alexander Bain's definition, which may be considered one of the essential sources of pragmatism: belief is a "readiness to act."[1] But this definition may be understood in two different ways. First, it may be said of beliefs founded on habit, as in the case of possible verifiability. "Take, for instance, yonder object on the wall. You and I consider it to be a 'clock,' altho no one of us has seen the hidden works that make it one. We let our notion pass for true without attempting to verify. . . . We *use* it as a clock, regulating the length of our lecture by it."[2] It is not at all a question of *knowing* if we are dealing with a clock; it suffices that everything happens as if we were dealing with a clock, and this belief disposes us to act. In this respect, we may say that the greater part of our daily lives goes exclusively on belief, not only because belief foresees, but also because it proceeds without verification. That something might be verifiable makes it *as if* verified, in keeping with the definition of this first sort of verification. We are already familiar with this first sense of the word "belief"; it designates solid beliefs, already established, founded on habit.

In the second instance, which is of greater interest to James, belief is still defined as a readiness to act, only it is no longer habit that provokes action; nothing provides any guarantee of the result. What then leads us to act? *Confidence*, or what James also calls faith. We believe when we can expect a result with some assurance. But to believe in a result that nothing guarantees requires faith beforehand.[3] In effect, we have no choice but to have faith. Put another way, faith is the necessary condition for belief when it ventures into the indeterminate, when it creates, in keeping with the second sort of verifiability (virtual). This does not mean that faith is a species of which belief is the genus. On the contrary, we cannot believe if we do not first feel faith. New ideas precede the habits we form from them. Faith is the condition—or rather the germ—of all belief. We act when we have faith in our motives, in our abilities, and in the coming of the world that will realize them.[4]

To believe is to foresee and wait. To have faith is to anticipate and hope. How do we know, for instance, if we are capable of leaping across a stream or not? It is not a matter of foreseeing but of anticipating, that is to say, of estimating through vague inquiries into the strength of our body, its state of relaxation, all the while eyeing the opposite bank for its firmness as well. Can we have faith in our body, in the stability of the rock, in the bank?[5] In contrast with habit, which is exercised in a determinate world, faith is paradoxically exercised in a world of indetermination, which James calls "the zone of formative processes, the dynamic belt of quivering uncertainty, the line where past and future meet."[6] From indetermination arises our need for faith, but because we have faith, we venture into the indeterminate.[7] Faith does not consist of realizing an action whose success is assured (foresight) but entails attempting an action whose outcome is uncertain (expectancy). It derives its energy from the obscure region where our power to act exceeds what we know of it.[8] The feeling of faith involves an experience of the domain of experimentation. It is thus the condition for any act of creation.

We need indetermination to have faith, as much as indetermination creates our need for faith. The indeterminate, or the virtual, is thus the milieu of our practice. Not only do we need faith in ourselves, we also need to believe in the world that presents itself to us. We need to believe in this world for all that is given. That the world is there, and I find myself included, is not enough. We are only dealing with the given substantiated by our senses. Faith is missing. This given must also contain something possible, and as James says, this possible must exceed the real, to the point where it is no longer a matter of being "in" the world but of acting "with" it to belong to it anew. Put another way, going beyond has two distinct orientations, one a matter of inferring something that is not given based on what is (tomorrow the sun will rise), another a matter of conferring meaning on what is given (somebody has a toothache; the clock gives the correct time); both are matters of interpreting signs. We may in fact doubt the given itself, or the meaning of this reality made up of signs. This is why the problem is, at the same time, less one of belief and more one of faith.

It sometimes happens that the given no longer has any meaning for the one who perceives it. This is not a matter of methodological doubt, however radical. Doubt clearly tells us what it is all about—a suspension of belief (but which hangs on to belief)—while a crisis of faith entails the destruction of belief. Belief becomes unmoored; the world ceases to have meaning. This is the first symptom of the crisis of faith. We are not "in" the world simply because of our perceptions of it. We are connected to it by our meanings, our goals. Without belief, perceptions are not enough to make us believe in this world, to make it meaningful. The tie that binds us to the world is thus extremely fragile. "Destroy this inner assurance, however, vague as it is, and all the light and radiance of existence is extinguished for these persons at a stroke. Often enough the wild-eyed look at life—the suicidal mood— will then set in."[9] All the connections tying us to the world are broken. The loss of connections, as in despair and morbid melancholy, is a secondary symptom.[10] Everything falls apart. The person remains sitting there "like a sort of sculptured Egyptian cat or Peruvian mummy."[11] All action becomes impossible. Faith is not the condition for "success"; it is vitality itself.

The impossibility of making meaning, of producing connections, of acting—that these three symptoms are inseparable is all too evident. It is because I am no longer able to give meaning to what I perceive that I am no longer connected to the world or able to act. We may assess the extent to which pragmatism prolongs psychology on these points. Action is not a simple reflex mechanism. We have seen that action is produced when a certain emotional threshold is crossed. To be precise, variations in the feeling of faith correspond to variations in intensity passing through the flow of consciousness. We have also seen that the rising or falling of intensity corresponds respectively to an enlargement or a shrinking of the field of consciousness (in fatigue, in melancholy). These variations are themselves sometimes abrupt (crisis), sometimes slow (lysis). Expressed in psychological terms, the crisis of faith thus involves an extreme drop in intensive flow and a shrinking of the field of consciousness or of its connections. This is why James tentatively addresses religious experience in terms of different degrees in the feeling of faith, by reference to different types of pessimism and optimism. In this way, James establishes a sort of scale as a function of thresholds crossed, moving from exhaustion to panicked terror at one end, and from hope to creative joy at the other.

Could it be that James finds in religion the solution permitting us to overcome such crises? James has often been defined as a theologian, as a "religious pragmatist." As some of his texts attest, his pragmatism may be taken as being, at heart, an apology for religious belief.[12] In fact, James does not rule out the idea that God may effectively act on certain souls. The idea of God lends itself to pragmatic critique, as does the idea of substance, or the idea of justice. James is a theologian only in this respect. He limits himself to an examination of the effects of the religious idea from a point of view that is at once psychological and pragmatic. Even more, the term "religion" in James is a generic term designating any belief in an invisible reality (as when we say of someone that justice is their religion, for instance).

But there is a more decisive reason confirming that James is not a theologian, or, we might do better to say, not merely or essentially a theologian. To be precise, what interests him is belief in this world, not belief in another world. Belief is atheist before it is religious. Those who are religious are not the only ones who may claim to believe, for religion is but one form of belief among many others. We are first believers in this world, even those of us who are religious. We may well wonder: Why, then, devote an entire work to religious experience? Will it not confirm that, despite the plurality of dogmas, belief remains narrowly religious? Therein lies a common paralogism: since God is accessible only through belief, it is assumed that God is the only object of belief. Yet, throughout *The Varieties of Religious Experience*, James not only provides numerous examples of atheist belief (in love, in art) as equivalents of religious faith, but also shows that the ground for religious belief is atheist.[13]

This is quite evident when James takes up the exemplary instance of conversion. We understand nothing of conversion when we take it as a passage from atheism to some religious doctrine or as a mere change in doctrine. Conversion is less opposed to atheism than it is to nihilism, in which there is no longer belief in anything, as when Tolstoy takes up the lament from Ecclesiastes, "all is vanity." Conversion assumes a passage through degree zero of affect and sensation, which destroys the feeling of faith.[14] While belief has to confront skepticism, faith, for its part, has to confront nihilism. Conversion is thus not specifically religious. Or, to be precise, religion is always ultimately atheist in its consequences.[15] It is never a matter of knowing whether the object of religious belief possesses reality or not. "The whole defence of religious faith hinges upon action."[16] It is less a matter of believing in a better world than of making this world better, even if it be through belief in another world.[17] As such, there is a secular ground for religion. Religion is one means among others for restoring the meaning of the world, of surmounting the nonmeaning provoked by moral crises.

The difficulty lies precisely in deploying new significations, venturing into new actions and new connections. Consequently, the world must be given to us a second time to establish in it new significations, as James's important distinction between "once born types" and "twice born types" attests. The soul undergoes a second birth when it surmounts the crisis of faith that has broken it. "The process is one of redemption, not of mere reversion to natural health, and the sufferer, when saved, is saved by what seems to him a second birth, a deeper kind of conscious being than he could enjoy before."[18] We no longer believe in the same way. We have lost a certain kind of faith, mixed with naïveté, credulity, and innocence. But in losing its first optimism, faith takes on new consistency. It is now based on other signs, or rather it establishes a relation with signs. We have to figure out which specific operation will allow us to broaden our power to act, or our horizons of thought.

Conventions: How to Choose a Philosophy

Whatever venture appears (crossing a stream, making a declaration of love, composing a sonata), it presents an attempt to make new connections. There is a first moment of assessment through which we make a vague evaluation of the situation. Diverse observations start to cohere within a given direction. The *conceived-of possible* is only a "living hypothesis" that refers back to *felt virtualities*. A first interpretation takes on consistency and determines the direction to take, yet without providing any guarantee for the result. Then comes a second moment in which we actually throw ourselves into action. Action consolidates a new idea and makes it tip over into a new situation. What has happened that we agree to act on the idea? Everything happens as if, in this second moment, we were making an agreement with the idea in order to act on it. This is what is properly called the act of faith. To have faith is to come to a tacit agreement. The agreement is tacit because, in a way, the idea promises nothing: we do not know in advance what will come of the agreement. This is why ideas or motivations for action must be called conventions, not only because they are signs (as we have already seen), but also because we grant them our faith. How else could we refer to what increases our power to act or to think, that is, what allows us to produce new connections or to consolidate an existing system, when we come into agreement with it (even if the agreement be informal, tacit, unperceived)? Faith is always faith in a convention that is in the making. Our power is indeed increased, since we pass from an indeterminate, dispersed, loose order to a determinate, organized, and consolidated order.[19]

Is this not precisely a definition of convention, an agreement without guarantee, which increases the power to act of those who make it, as the famous example of the oarsmen in Hume illustrates?[20] The idea has a conventional aspect to it insofar as it enlarges the field of consciousness and, correlatively, increases our power to act. We make agreements with concepts, sometimes provisional, sometimes definite; or rather, we experiment to find out which ones agree or do not agree with what we are doing. Was it not thus already by convention that we admitted that we were dealing with a clock because it allowed us to track time throughout the lesson? The particular moment when we place our faith in a series of uncertain signs may be called a convention; convention is defined as a tacit agreement with an idea that is indeterminate (at least with respect to its consequences) in accordance to which we venture into action with a sense of faith.

This is the case with religion. Religious faith appeals not to a determinate faculty but to the indetermination in our power to act. It appeals to new regions, subconscious forces of our consciousness, what James calls "invasive" experience. Fields of consciousness alternate to let visions enter, as well as delirium and violent shifts in personality, which remain inexplicable through inquiries based on clear unperturbed consciousness.

The theologian's contention that the religious man is moved by an external power is vindicated, for one of the peculiarities of invasions from the subconscious region is that they take on objective appearances, and suggest to the Subject an external control. In the religious life the control is felt as "higher"; but since on our hypothesis it is primarily the higher faculties of our own hidden mind which are controlling, the sense of union with the power beyond us is a sense of something, not merely apparently, but literally true.[21]

James says that we may call such unconscious forces God if we like. We do not take leave of the immanence of the flow of consciousness; on the contrary, we explore and expand it. Religion liberates in us unheard-of possibilities that faith actualizes. The value of religion in this respect is precisely that it expands our mental horizon and our power to act. James never stops saying that what characterizes religion is the passage from contraction to expansion of the field of consciousness. Once again, connections with the world are possible; the world is given again, enlarged and renewed, replenished with possibilities. In this sense, our relation with religion is a relation of convention insofar as religion augments our power to act. We may, if we like, call the powers we actualize God, but that is still by convention.[22]

We may say that everything is conventional, from the formation of concepts to their usage, *even including perceptions themselves*. To perceive is natural, but our perceptions are conventional in that they interpret shocks of experience. Even with perceptions, agreements are made in that there is always more going on than perceiving: we anticipate, evaluate, interpret. A convention is a sign that engages us in a practice likely to produce meaning, to increase our power of action, to develop connections in accordance with a tendency or given finality, such as perception. That everything is conventional does not mean that there is no more nature. It means that natural functions are distributed into multiple conventions. Bergson's formulation is apt here: to have habits is natural, but the habits we adopt are not natural.[23] Or that of Hume: to construct is natural, but our constructions are not natural.[24] Similarly James might well say, We are by nature curious, but we become researchers by convention. If he gives education an important place (he devoted two works to it), it is precisely because it shows how natural instincts enter into conventions. The flow of the stream of consciousness is oriented toward new meanings that increase the expanse of its field and its powers of thought. Education forms, through habit, new sensorimotor schemata such that instincts and tendencies are displaced, complicated, amplified.[25] In other words, the art of pedagogy consists of producing a more complex reaction or a substitute reaction that agrees with a more general context as a result of a series of intermediary assemblages (such as punishment) that then disappear, shortcutted, abridged.

Conventionalism is by definition inseparable from a pluralist philosophy. As Eugène Dupréel observes, when the same force holds sway over all individuals, it is utterly impossible to speak of convention. On the other hand, when a unique order is contested by the appearance of another, the two orders then appear as conventions.[26] Or to build on Henri Poincaré's remarks, it is because there are new geometric spaces that Euclidean space no longer appears to be natural, but rather becomes conventional.[27] When we declare that three-dimensional Euclidean space, or the clock over the door, is convention, what do we mean? Have we not fallen into certain arbitrariness? If our relation with concepts is conventional, if concepts themselves are conventions, this assumes of course that, while we are making an agreement with such and such a concept, it might have been otherwise. The limit of conventionalism is its negation by necessity. How do we declare that we are free to make agreements with concepts or to implement a decree when we clearly have no choice? How can something that bears the force of law be called a simple rule unless the agreement is precisely not to recognize what specifically makes it necessary?

What are the reasons that make us "choose" Euclidean space? Like James, Poincaré affirms that we choose Euclidean space based on convenience. Our choice, among all possible conventions, is guided by experimental facts: one geometry cannot be truer than another; it can only be handier because (1) it is simpler, and (2) it agrees well with the properties of natural solids.[28] We may claim that resemblance or agreement support the truth of a hypothesis, but the essential lies elsewhere since utility makes us seek resemblance. Necessity is not denied; it is only displaced. It is no longer an intrinsic property of the idea or of reasoning; it is now rooted in the motivations that produce resemblance or agreement: utility, functionality, practical interest, or aesthetic interest.

It might be supposed that James, as a pragmatist, would choose based on utility—according to a simplistic definition of pragmatism, he would opt for a philosophy, a theory, a hypothesis that would work, that would enjoy "success." James feels, however, that solutions or rules are immanent in each case and are not dependent on values transcending existences. It is not possible to set up any universal rule.

There are higher and lower limits of possibility set to each personal life. If a flood but goes above one's head, its absolute elevation becomes a matter of small importance; and when we touch our own upper limit and live in our own highest centre of energy, we may call ourselves saved, no matter how much higher someone else's centre may be. A small man's salvation will always be a great salvation and the greatest of all facts *for him*.[29]

It is impossible to determine in advance what kind of convention may prove satisfactory for a particular individual at a particular moment. Yes, we must choose, but each of us for herself, depending on the situation. The situation is not arbitrary but rooted in a necessity that is by its nature mobile and changing. Thus James, for instance, latches onto verses of Scripture when he undergoes his crisis of "ontological terror," yet he is not led toward a religious life. The agreement is momentary and does not last beyond the resolution of the crisis. Likewise, we may move through conventions that have nothing glorious or functional about them, that may sometimes even destroy us instead of guaranteeing us success, American style.

In other words, pragmatism is a method of practical evaluation of conventions. The question proper to the pragmatic method may now be formulated as follows: With what ideas may we move from conventions, to augment and consolidate our feeling of faith, to enlarge our field of action or our field of thought? This method applies particularly to philosophy, not by virtue of its presumed dignity or some sort speculative superiority, but because we always act according to a "philosophy" in the more ordinary sense than what the term formally indicates. In this looser sense, a philosophy is simply a system of beliefs that determines thinking and acting. Every philosophy thus becomes a practical philosophy.

It may be objected that a clear distinction is needed between theoretical activity and practical activity, between what a person can know and what a person must do. Yet this is precisely the divide pragmatism rejects. Both entail concepts that must be interpreted in terms of their practical finality. This is even true of concepts whose usage seems purely theoretical, such as the concept of substance, but also that of totality, necessity, and consciousness. Any concept, even the most technical, even the most scholarly, harbors a practical interest in that it refers to different possibilities for acting and thinking. My conduct is not the same if I conceive of myself as an ego than if I see myself as a flow of thought, because the possible consequences that ensue are not the same, in practical terms. Put otherwise, to affirm or to deny the existence of an ego is already a practical or moral decision rather than purely theoretical or epistemological. This is all the more true when conceiving of worlds. How is it possible to imagine that we can engage in theoretical debates on the question of nature without at the same time drawing out the practical consequences in which each hypothesis implicates us? The question of whether an idea is theoretically true is of little importance compared to the question of whether it practically gives rise to possibilities for our future action.

The question bears on the meaning of the idea, of the theory under consideration. From the point of view of pragmatism, what gives meaning to a statement is not its correspondence with a given state of things but rather what we may expect or hope of it, the action or thought to which it leads. Meaning thus lies in practical consequences, in keeping with the pragmatic definition of truth. Take, for instance, the classical controversy about the concept of substance.[30] We may either posit the existence of a substance with attributes or deny its existence and retain only the cohesiveness of attributes, which alone are knowable. Each of the two theses, radically opposed, implies different consequences, one leading to spiritualism (which James associates with theism), and the other to materialism. Yet it makes no difference whether we believe that the world was the result of a material assemblage or the work of a divine mind. How can it make no difference whether we choose one thesis or another from a theoretical point of view? Whichever of the two theses is adopted, what makes for its truth is that it holds for the past state of the universe as well as for its present and future state.[31] To claim, however, that truth preexists the states of things yet to come means that the future already belongs to the past. We may say no more of the future in question than that it will have been true.[32] In this respect, the claims of these two doctrines are entirely retrospective. "Whatever the details of experience may prove to be, *after the fact of them* the absolute will adopt them. It is an hypothesis that functions retrospectively only, not prospectively."[33]

Theism and materialism are both concerned with the past of the universe. The world is already complete, and the system containing it is definitively closed. Consequently, whichever of the two hypotheses we choose, the world remains the same. It matters little then to know who or what produced a finished world. The future is already exhausted; it has already given what it can give. What is more, if the choice makes no difference, the dispute is in vain. From a pragmatist point of view, *theism and materialism mean exactly the same thing*: "Then let the pragmatist be asked to choose between their theories. . . . Both theories have shown all their consequences and, by the hypothesis we are adopting, these are identical. The pragmatist must consequently say that the two theories, in spite of their different-sounding names, mean exactly the same thing, and that the dispute is purely verbal."[34] Once again, the value of a concept or a theory is not measured by its truth; on the contrary, its truth is measured by the possibilities that it generates for future action.[35] James thus proposes to reverse the primacy of past over future, to make theory into a moment of practice, and not the inverse. "What is this world going to be? What is life eventually to make of itself? The center of gravity of philosophy must therefore alter its place."[36] We do not seek a philosophy in which to believe, but a philosophy that makes us believe, that liberates new possibilities. Such is the ambition of James's method. He never tires of saying, rather like Kierkegaard, that we need something that lets us breathe. The faculties of belief were not given to us "to make orthodoxies and heresies withal; they were given us to live by."[37] To a certain extent, philosophy must play a role analogous to that of religion: to give us reasons to believe in the world.

What exactly makes radical empiricism superior to other philosophies? The answer is not guaranteed, because, after all, it may be preferable to believe in the existence of a substantial self than in the existence of a flow of transitory thoughts. There is no criterion that will allow us to make an absolute choice for empiricism rather than rationalism or intellectualism, theism rather than materialism. Absolutism undoubtedly offers a safer haven. The pluralism of radical empiricism usually arouses skepticism and doubt rather than a feeling of faith and a taste for adventure. Isn't it pluralism that breeds mistrust and doubt in the first place? James readily admits that this is the case:

> This forms one permanent inferiority of pluralism from the pragmatic point of view. It has no saving message for incurably sick souls. Absolutism, among its other messages, has that message, and is the only scheme that has it necessarily. That constitutes its chief superiority and is the source of its religious power. . . . The needs of sick souls are surely the most urgent; and believers in the absolute should rather hold it to be great merit in their philosophy that it can meet them so well. The pragmatism or pluralism which I defend has

to fall back on a certain ultimate hardihood, a certain willingness to live without assurances or guarantees. . . . Which side is right here, who can say?[38]

The question is no longer "what makes radical empiricism or pluralism superior?" but "for whom is it suited?" Who may have need of empiricism? Whom may it serve? On this head, James offers a sketch of an essentially dualist typology, of sick souls versus healthy souls; and yet *The Varieties of Religious Experience* shows that such a typology lends itself to an entire series of intermediate degrees. The sick soul needs to attach itself to stable established dogmas. The need for safety is substituted for a feeling of faith. In contrast, the healthy soul ventures into the indeterminate, without guarantee or certainty. We should not conclude, however, that pluralism and absolutism are equal in value. These passages from James deliberately underscore that absolutism does not prove capable of increasing our feeling of faith. It is only capable of solidifying it within a more paralyzing demand, for *security*. Absolutism, then, may ultimately engender mistrust. It does indeed make us believe but does not allow us to establish new connections with the world, or to create new meanings.

I have argued that radical empiricism needs pragmatism as a method permitting it to sustain its strict focus on functions; but now we see how pragmatism requires radical empiricism for individuals to conceive of their lives as a process of creation. Therein lies radical empiricism's practical destiny as philosophy. It may now be easier to understand why it is essentially presented as a liberating enterprise; it brings us the raw materials for a world to make. This is why James, like Bergson, requires an open world, "with doors and windows open to possibilities uncontrollable in advance."[39] We need an unstable, indeterminate world. When we believe in what is possible, we conceive of those possibles within a world in which there is something virtual. The theoretical point of view is, in essence, incapable of giving us faith since it invariably thinks in a closed world. We need exteriority. The exteriority of relations is one of the essential conditions for faith to the extent that it appeals to our power to create. It is only with that sort of world that we are able to move about, producing actions and connections. "In the each-form, on the contrary, a thing may be connected by intermediary things, with a thing with which it has no immediate or essential connexion. It is thus at all times in many possible connexions which are not necessarily actualized at the moment."[40]

The problem with pessimism, as well as with optimism, is that the world is considered as a collective All, lost or saved a priori.

> We *must* take one of four attitudes in regard to the other powers: either 1. Follow intellectualist advice: wait for evidence; and while waiting, do nothing; or 2. *Mistrust* the other powers and, sure that the universe will fail, *let* it fail; or 3. *Trust* them; and at any rate do *our* best, in spite of the *if*; or, finally, 4. *Flounder*, spending one day in one attitude, another day in another. . . . The 3rd way seems the only wise way. . . . Only through our precursive trust in it can it [the pluralist world] come into being.[41]

Pluralism calls on the faith of each individual. Pluralism is neither pessimistic nor optimistic but melioristic. The advantage of meliorism, a term James borrows from George Eliot, is to assume that, if the world is open, it can be made better. It thus calls on the active will of each person insofar as our salvation, in this very world, is not guaranteed, and it can only happen if we contribute to it individually. In this way, we live in the *same* world; we develop relations to it, actions and meanings that interfere with or complement one another, according to the conjunctions passed through, or the disjunctions encountered. In this way, we form a community.

Community of Interpretation

I would like here to venture a hypothesis. It seems, in effect, that James's conventionalism is inseparable from a thinking of community whose features need to be specified. At no point does James call explicitly on the notion of community, as does Peirce, for instance, who invokes a community of researchers on the horizon of semiology, as well as Royce, who calls on a vast community of interpretation, and Dewey, who proposes a model of liberal democratic community. At no point does James invoke any particular social model; and yet when he affirms that pragmatism is a democratic philosophy, he is not referring only to each person's freedom of judgment.[42] Likewise, when he says that pluralism, more than any other philosophy, is a social philosophy, because connections do the work, this is not merely a metaphor.[43] Without a doubt, the social world provides James with a model, as he suggests elsewhere.[44]

Thus far we have acted as if the conventional relation linked the individual to a series of signs through which it constructs its world. Yet, to the extent to which it passes through signs, convention also passes through other individuals with whom we come to an agreement as to the meaning of these signs. In other words, I do not come to an agreement on signs without at the same time coming to a virtual agreement with other individuals who have also come to an agreement on the same signs. What is in question, then, is less the individual than the relation that links two individuals. It is not individuals that come first, but the signs they exchange. James is very close to Tarde here. In light of the many parallels between the two works, it makes sense that James would profess a great admiration for Tarde's sociology.[45] Is it not indeed Tarde who declares that sociology must call on psychology, not intracerebral but intercerebral psychology, which would study "the rise of conscious relations between two or more individuals"?[46]

Tarde explains that the relation of a subject with another is the relationship of one sensation with another sensation, one will with another will, a belief with another belief; simply put, the person perceiving is reflected in the other, by way of a mental transmission—and that relation is primary, for, between two individuals, a belief acts on another belief, on gestures, postures, intonations, and so forth. Like Tarde, James states, "Our faith is faith in someone else's faith, and in the greatest matters this is most the case."[47] There is indeed always a social background to any convention as the individual is made of interindividual relations. Society is what forces me to adopt certain conventions, to believe in certain ones rather than others. We are constrained on every side. But the social constraint above all is the most essential and powerful, first because other constraints develop within it, and subsequently because it conditions other conventions—including our construction of reality—and finally because it is the one that regulates our beliefs.

Under such conditions, it is odd that James's philosophy has been reproached for its lack of a social dimension.[48] Generally, this deficit has been explained with reference to his individualism. But what does this mean? Does this mean that James does not propose any collective salvation? Such a reason is not sufficient. With James, and later with Dewey, contrary to what has often been said, the individual is an immediately social reality. It is absurd to think that James's individualism prevented the development of a social or sociological dimension because it is precisely society that forms individuals. This does not mean that society is presupposed, given in advance as a totality within which individualities must be introduced; neither does it mean that James does not attach any importance to the question of society. Rather, he thinks of society as integrated into diverse streams of consciousness through which it is ceaselessly made, and to be made. The way in which individuals are made in society is the basis for knowing how society is made through them. Therein lies the significance of the phrase "the individual is directly social."

> Thus social evolution is a resultant of the interaction of two wholly distinct factors—the individual, deriving his peculiar gifts from the play of physiological and infra-social forces, but bearing all the power of initiative and origination in his hands; and, second, the social environment, with its power of adopting or rejecting both him and his gifts. Both factors are essential for change. The community stagnates without the impulse of the individual. The impulse dies away without the sympathy of the community.[49]

Tarde's two social quantities may be found in the above passage, desire as power of invention, and belief as power of organization or selection.[50] Put otherwise, the development of the individual is inseparable from the social development to which the individual contributes. Society is integrated within the consciousness of individuals; in this manner, individuals are integrated into society.

The individual develops within these institutions that guide and orient her flow of consciousness, as we have already seen in education. To educate is to provide access to established meanings, to already shaped conventions, to common sense. Education is this modulating and variable movement that consolidates flows of belief. As belief is specified, it is spread and fortified; it is born of the social world. *Common sense*, this ancient ground of habits, is inseparable from the *sense of community*. The beliefs of a community and, consequently, the community itself hold together through such sense. It is a social memory analogous to what Tarde calls imitation.

Common sense here plays a determining role: for the meanings that make up reality are largely already established conventions that each consciousness appropriates in turn, which perpetuates the stability of social forms and orients the unstable flows of beliefs. To repeat, we do not believe whatever we want: we usually believe what others believe or what serves the interest of the State to have us believe, and then the sign becomes a sign of power or, to follow Tarde's terms, a "magnetic passkey." As James states, prestige may make us believe: it is "not insight but the *prestige* of the opinions, is what makes the spark shoot from them and light up our sleeping magazines of faith. . . . Our belief in truth itself, for instance, that there is a truth, and that our minds and it are made for each other—what is it but a passionate affirmation of desire, in which our social system backs us up?"[51] The essence of the social link consists of making us believe, of emitting signs that make us believe, that make us act and think in a determinate way, that stabilize a belief. This is the role of religion, of philosophy, of ideas in general, such as we have explained them. To say that we believe in an idea is an incomplete description of the phenomenon of belief. As Tarde states, in terms quite similar to those of James, "But does not belief in anyone always mean belief in that which he believes or seems to believe? Does not obedience to someone mean that we will that which he wills or seems to will?"[52]

Already we sense that a society is a set of multiple conventions, definitive or provisional, general or local. Belief is stabilized through them, either in the *sedimentation* of idea-habits, or in the *consolidation* of a new idea. So it is that each of us operates through conventions without it being necessary to postulate a collective association. This allows for determining with greater precision how relations of faith are established with others. We come into agreement about meanings even though the agreement is not explicitly established. As James says, signs suffice because they refer back to virtualities. When we deal with others, the question of faith then becomes, Can I believe what a person wants me to believe? As in the case of religion and philosophy, assessment proceeds through a sort of intuitive and vague evaluation of the indeterminate. The relation with an other is a relation of reverberation, to use James's and Royce's terms, or a reflecting relation, to use Tarde's. An other is not my likeness in the sense in which we would see ourselves in the other. The other is not thought on the model of resemblance. The other is neither *alter ego* nor *analogon*, but neither is the other an unknowable Other: the distance between us is only that of the signs emitted. If it were a matter of resemblance, it would depend on actuals, actual traits, feature by feature. Yet, what bring us into relation are virtualities. It is not possible for virtualities to resemble one another since they are indeterminate, whence sympathy.[53] We have a wealth of virtualities in common. Community but not resemblance. We *have* things in common rather than *being* in resemblance. We have properties in common and not qualities that resemble one another.

Before any definite engagement, a relation of faith is established with the other, which does not bear on anything determinate. It is not a matter of a contract with its determinate clauses spurring faith, but rather a relation of indeterminate faith leading to determination of a convention, when it takes place. How can a social organism subsist? James asks, Is it not because each individual is convinced that others are carrying out their duties as I am carrying out mine?

> A social organism of any sort whatever, large or small, is what it is because each member proceeds to his own duty with a trust that the other members will simultaneously do theirs. Wherever a desired result is achieved by the co-operation of many independent persons, its existence as a fact is a pure consequence of the pre-cursive *faith* in one another of those immediately concerned. A government, an army, a commercial system, a ship, a college, an athletic team, all exist on this condition, without which not only is nothing achieved, but nothing is even attempted.[54]

The question of social cohesiveness does not depend on respect for external collective constraints but on a faith that is distributed within the community. The notion of convention must thus be substituted for that of contract. While the *contract* determines its content through a limitation of powers, the *convention* calls on the indeterminate to actualize itself through rules that are established along the way. As such, the convention is a means of increasing the power of those who function through it, as James illustrates with an example: the alliance of train robbers. He asks, How can they succeed despite their scant number? Because they can count on one another while the train's passengers, suspicious of one another, cannot.[55] Society must therefore be thought on the basis of relations of faith and belief working across individuals.

When association is conceived of from the collective point of view, it takes the form of a contract, but when it is conceived of from the distributive point of view, it takes the form of a convention. Contractualist theories make the point clearly; the contract calls on the people as a collectivity. As such, in Rousseau for instance, we pass from natural dispersion to the unity of a general will, the constitution of a people as a collective unity. By the same token, the people are represented by a sovereign and legitimate unity, precisely what Rousseau calls "a collective being."[56] Contrary to appearances, Rousseau's point of departure is not a distributive treatment (even if each one of us adopts the contract) but an atomist postulate that makes us pass from the individual to the society, from the part to the whole. We here discover the basic feature of all thought of the contract: the absorption of the multiple into the collective One-All. We do not need, however, to pass from the individual to society because, as Dewey says, the individual is an immediately social reality. This is what Hume had already said: society comes first.

This opposition between a collective treatment and a distributive treatment of society is, of course, prolonged in the opposition between Durkheim's sociology and Tarde's. It is precisely in the name of individual differences that James rejects contemporary sociology because he finds that it does not call on the forces of the individual. "And I for my part cannot but consider the talk of the contemporary sociological school about averages and general laws and predetermined tendencies, with its obligatory undervaluing of the importance of individual differences, as the most pernicious and immoral of fatalisms. Suppose there is a social equilibrium fated to be, whose is it to be—that of your preference, or mine? There lies the question of questions, and it is one which no study of averages can decide."[57]

Therein lies James's hypothesis, which is also the general principle of Tarde's works: work based on infrapersonal and interindividual psychology will be the more sociological for it. Tarde also rejects Durkheim's notion of the "collective social fact." The social fabric is shot through with processes, with imitations, counter-imitations, and inventions, which are born of individuals' brains through the crisscrossing of infraindividual flows. Tarde and James are in agreement in their opposition to the idea of a collective treatment of social realities. The central concepts invoked by Tarde, of imitation, opposition, and invention, effectively undergo a rigorously distributive treatment. It is each individual who, on her own account, imitates, opposes, and invents (although each individual is herself permeated with infraindividual flows). Resemblances are not fused into a vast "social fact" that totalizes them.[58] According to Tarde, they are propagated through the social fabric, sometimes acting continuously from one person to the next, swept along as in a hurricane, or sometimes jumping over persons and striking in a more disparate manner as in an epidemic, or sometimes as an insurrection that develops even more freely, following the swiftest network, such as the telegraph, the train, and so forth. Imitation appears not only as an action but as "a generation at a distance," associated with the appearance of the great network infrastructures.[59] Opposition is not between the individual and the social as in Durkheim but between the collective (macrological) and the distributive (micrological). For this reason, James praises Tarde as a worthy successor to Darwin for his attention to "tiny differences" and individual variations. His admiration is inseparable from a political opposition to the power of greatness, as James beautifully underscores in these passages:

> As for me, my bed is made: I am against bigness & greatness in all their forms; and with the invisible molecular moral forces that work from individual to individual, stealing in through the crannies of this world like so many soft rootlets or like the capillary oozing of water, and yet rending the hardest monuments of man's pride, if you give them time. The bigger the unit you deal with, the hollower, the more brutal, the more mendacious is the life displayed. So I am against all big organizations as such, national ones first and foremost, against all big successes and big results, and in favor of the eternal forces of truth which always work in the individual and immediately unsuccessful way, underdogs always, till history comes after they are long dead, and puts them on the top.[60]

Immense streams bearing multiple beliefs flow through communities of individuals. I do not believe in signs without believing that others also believe in them as well. I believe in a belief. We believe and we make believe. Epistemology is established on a social basis, as a condition of our semiotic conventions.

> In the last analysis, then, we believe that we all know and think about and talk about the same world, because *we believe our percepts are possessed by us in common.* . . . What I am for you is in the first instance a percept of your own. Unexpectedly, however, I open and show you a book, uttering certain sounds the while. These acts are also your percepts, but they so resemble acts of yours with feelings prompting them, that you cannot doubt I have the feelings too, or that the book is one book felt in both our worlds.[61]

The world only has meaning if it is produced between two monads that are interpreting. It is thus not a matter of a mutual submission to a general law since nothing preexists the relation. It is a matter of an implicit accord. A convention is a *rule of interpretation* that is established in the course of exchanging signs. The real is essentially a social convention, not only because the two monads together determine it as real, but also because they operate on it in a similar manner. As such, reality (even taken in the epistemological sense) is essentially a set of objects and relations of a social nature.

Does James not ultimately assume a grand community of interpretation similar to the one Josiah Royce presents in *The Problem of Christianity*? In terms much like those of James, Royce asks, How can interpretation further the faith of individuals in one another? Each interpretation requires a sign, and conversely, each sign calls for an interpretation. As with Peirce, the process of interpretation is unlimited; but, in contrast with Peirce, Royce conceives it as being above all social in that it is addressed to other consciousnesses. "By itself, the process of interpretation calls, in ideal, for an infinite sequence of interpretations. For every interpretation, being addressed to somebody, demands interpretation from the one to whom it is addressed."[62] The sign to interpret, the interpreter, and the mind to which the interpretation is addressed: this is Royce's trinity. If the goal of interpretation is attained, the sign becomes intelligible for the person for whom it was interpreted. Any statement calls on a community: "Whoever says, 'I have discovered a physical fact,' is not merely reporting the workings of his own individual ideas. . . . He is therefore appealing to a community of interpretation."[63] A "community of interpretation," turned toward an ideal, toward the spiritual unity of the community, may be born of this mutual comprehension.[64]

To the extent that our connections are interpretations, and that interpretations never cease to increase connections in proportion to our feeling of faith, may we not see across the entire body of James's philosophy the implicit presence of communities of interpretation, since even James continually appeals to a world in the making? We must establish the new meanings, new acts, and new connections for it. We have to believe in beliefs, and that is why faith is necessary, and interpretations are by rights unlimited. With Royce, under the sway of a certain relation, individuals may serve a cause superior to them, which is brought about socially even while being suprasocial. Individuals may be melded together within a communal cause. With James, on the contrary, signs are not over and above us as ideal causes that abolish the distance between those who serve them; signs are *between us*, in a relation of immanence. As his brother, the novelist Henry James, said to one of his friends, "Do not melt too much into the universe."[65] The social relation remains by definition an action at a distance, conventional, and not a feeling of melding. *The unity of agreement does not reduce the multiplicity of ways of entering into relation with it.* This is why we may equally well say that communities are multiple, according to the signs with which they are in agreement, and according to whether they withdraw into mistrust (security) or open into faith. Here we return to the idea of a mosaic philosophy, which proved an inspiration for the Chicago School of Sociology.[66]

Conclusion

To dissociate James from broader movements affecting the entire United States as well as the political and social models that spurred discussion among contemporary thinkers may seem quite difficult. Pragmatism undoubtedly marked the culmination of a break with transcendentalism. Certainly, James holds onto certain aspects of it when he invokes the necessity of faith in relation to self, to the world, and to others; this does not mean that its coordinates were not modified. Faith is now exercised in a pluralist world whose bits cannot be blended into a harmonious All or Whole (whence James's reservations about the Hegelianism of Royce and especially of Bradley). In transcendentalism, faith is diffused through the Whole formed by Nature-God and human society, in a glorious pantheism. It is a matter of a priori faith in the Whole of the universe. In contrast, what pragmatism demonstrates is that relations are irreducibly exterior and, consequently, cannot be melded together. What pragmatism in general calls for are multiple semiological communities whose rules of interpretation are elaborated along the way in an immanent manner— Loyalism in Royce, the scientific community of researchers in Peirce, liberal democracy in Dewey, each of them presents, in their way, a definitive break with transcendentalism. American political thought in this respect does have its specificity. It is no longer a matter of a community of believers, a new Church, as was still the case with the religious communities and Fourierist phalansteries of the first colonies, and as was still the case with the transcendentalists, although in the form of faith-based community. Sympathy takes the place of charity, much as faith takes the place of belief.

What a renewed form of pragmatism proposes is for the community to regulate the relations of interpretation and the statements inseparable from them. Thus Rorty comes to claim affiliation with James or Dewey or even Peirce, and to propose a "neo-pragmatism" insofar as he defines the search for truth less as a rational procedure than as a desire for intersubjective consensus. "For pragmatists, the desire for objectivity is not the desire to escape the limitations of one's community, but simply the desire for as much intersubjective agreement as possible, the desire to extend the reference of 'us' as far as we can."[1] Such a conclusion appears all the more justified in that all four writers invoke consensus as one of the essential aspects of community. According to Peirce, consensus is the community of opinion in which any rational agent may participate, or, to use James's expression, "one great stage of equilibrium in the human mind's development, the stage of *common sense*."[2] Yet this stage of consensus, which in James simply describes social memory, cannot be taken as an end in itself, as is the case in Rorty. In consensus, Rorty finds an indigenous trait: we represent one another. He proposes, in this regard, a new model of conversation whose singular merit is to clearly reveal its disturbing ambition to achieve consensus. Can we accept, however, the way in which Rorty reduces the notion of community to "our community, the community of liberal intellectuals of the modern secular West"? How to accept that he is able to say, in the name of neo-pragmatism, "We Western liberal intellectuals should accept the fact that we have to start from where we are, and that this means there are lots of views we simply cannot take seriously."[3] We reasonable and conscientious men, we who have a sense of liberal and democratic values, we pursue the great conversation inaugurated by Socrates and perpetuated until it reached us today. Who will appear who is not in agreement with us, with our values of Justice, Equality, Fairness, and Truth?

One of the major misinterpretations of convention is indeed conceiving of it as consensus, as with the model of conversation Rorty proposes. What exactly is consensus? It is the production of statements that cannot be contradicted, or if they are, will lead back to a discussion whose parameters are predefined. It entails the production of statements within an ultimately predefined framework. We may not agree but we are at least in agreement about communicating reasonably. The challenge presented by contradiction leads not to the nature of the concept and its logical or practical liaisons, but to an intersubjective and communicational agreement. Yet we find absolutely no trace of convention since there is not the least increase in the power of our theoretical or practical activity, but at best the makings of generalities (and the singular trick used to justify these consensual generalities is to come up with extremist adversaries who contest them). The prehensive increase of a concept or an action is here confused with the extension of a generality. The more general is the agreement, the more consensual it appears. But the more conventional is the agreement, the more it gains in consolidation (which does not preclude it being general, as is the case with social or political conventions that depend on common interests).

It all comes down to defining conversation as an extension of indigenous values, a sort of imperialism wherein Western opinion is the unique source of values. Ethnocentrism—defended by Rorty—profoundly contradicts the inherent pluralism of pragmatism, not to mention the creative approach to seeking consensus for which pragmatism wishes to provide a method. In Rorty's texts, we find the disconcerting features of the ethnos, of mutual recognition among representatives of the same community of thought. It is useless then to proclaim nobly that community does not depend on national or racial traits; it is in vain to declare that it is all a matter of rational community; once we treat these national or racial traits as a matter of reason, there is no going back.

Once again, I would like to say that it is impossible to make pragmatism into a philosophy of economic or political opportunism, or to reduce it to such vague definitions as "a sense of action" or "a taste for the concrete," which is ultimately what Rorty serves up in a renewed form, for the exportation of liberal values through communication. Pragmatism does not set up success or failure as the alternatives, as has often been claimed, but rather presents salvation or loss. Faith is a vital matter. "Refuse to believe, and you shall indeed be right, for you shall irretrievably perish. But believe, and again you shall be right, for you shall save yourself. You make one or the other of two possible universes true by your trust or mistrust."[4] It is not the philosophy of the businessperson or of liberalism, even in the form of "communicational transactions." It is the philosophy of the ordinary person who must believe in this world, which is also a world of business. The crisis of faith is the sign of those who despair of believing in this world. Nothing succeeds in making them act or hope any longer. A new philosophy is then necessary. Functionalism is also made for what ceases to function.

Afterword: Diversity as Method

Thomas Lamarre

Contemporary scientists often cite the work of William James with approval. In *Self Comes to Mind*, for instance, when neuroscientist Antonio Damasio addresses questions about how the brain constructs a mind and how the brain makes that mind conscious, he builds directly on James's *Principles of Psychology* (1890):

> James thought that the self-as-object, the material me, was the sum total of all a man could call his. . . . I agree. But James also thought something else with which I am in even greater agreement: what allows the mind to know that such dominions exist and belong to their mental owners—body, mind, past and present, and all the rest—is that the perception of any of these items generates emotions and feelings, and in turn, the feelings accomplish the separation between the contents that belong to the self and those that do not. From my perspective, such feelings operate as markers.[1]

Likewise, when scientists pose questions about religion, or when scientific approaches to religion are in question, James's name frequently crops up, again with appreciation. Neurologist James H. Austin's efforts to understand the practice of zen meditation in neurophysiological terms are a prime example.[2] In such instances, however, James's *Varieties of Religious Experience* (1902) is usually cited.

While contemporary scientific references to James draw on his work in diverse ways, it is nonetheless evident that the appeal of James today derives in no small part from his willingness to take up questions about consciousness and experience as posed scientifically. James's reputation comes of his commitment to thinking with and through the sciences. Nonetheless, with some notable exceptions, scientific writing that draws on James tends to avoid some of the thornier philosophical problems raised in his work. Its focus is usually on *The Principles of Psychology* and *The Varieties of Religious Experience*, while the later essays published in *Radical Empiricism* (1912) are largely ignored. In contrast, the new surge of interest in James in the humanities in North America tends to call on the full range of his work, and with greater emphasis on his radical empiricism, even casting the earlier work in the light of the later. Yet here, too, James's reputation for taking the sciences seriously remains palpable, and the renewed engagement with his work has arisen primarily among scholars interested in the sciences, especially within science and technology studies and media studies.

Thus, when William Connolly turns to recent neuroscience research on the plasticity of brain processes to introduce "rich mixtures of affective energy and intersubjective processes" into the domain of political theory, he deals at length with William James, showing how his layered, or multitiered, approach to consciousness paves the way for a renewed and expanded conceptualization of pluralism.[3] More surprising perhaps is the evocation of James in studies of wireless signal processing, networks, and computational architectures. In Adrian Mackenzie's account of the proliferation of signal processing, for instance, he draws both on James's "waveform-based understanding of experience to expand the envelope of relations comprising experience" and his notion of conjunctive relations to describe how the world hangs together.[4]

In the wake of Mackenzie's work, the impact of James on media studies has expanded. Central to Anna Munster's bid for a relational and processual understanding of data and networks are James's concepts of "concatenated union" and "withness."[5] She argues, for instance, "If, for James, the barest of relations to be accounted for within a philosophy of radical empiricism is 'withness' . . . then the relational database might be considered the technical instantiation of just such a concatenated enumeration of life. The relational database foregrounds the 'relations' that organize data, making these the actual *stuff* of databasing."[6] Thus, she concludes that data and networks are "intensively accidental—contesting, contingent, conjunctive—yet extensively regulated fields."[7]

In a similar way, James's insistence that thought is not in the brain but in transition spurs Luciana Parisi to pinpoint the shortcomings of the neurosensorial model of thought (or neural connectionism) in the context of computation, showing that it only takes into account "the mutual connections between the world and the brain, between interior and exterior." The neurosensorial model entirely ignores the "algorithmic prehension of infinite qualities"[8] It is not able to deal with the "contagious architecture of these quantic infinities [that] turns the computational grid into a Swiss cheese of irregular holes, rough edges, and blind spots."[9]

What is striking about the entrance of radical empiricism into accounts of media, networks, and computation is the degree to which "withness" comes to the fore—concatenated, connective, conjunctive, contagious. Initially, this emphasis might be taken for a side effect of the subject matter (networks and computation), and yet Connolly, too, winds up calling on James's notion of "protean connectionism."[10]

The emphasis on withness within this new "science and media" take on James is especially timely and welcome, because James's work has often met with rebuke for its tendency to rely on the individual. James's philosophy has often been accused of lacking a social dimension. His willingness to address the individual in isolation has often been mistaken for methodological individualism, even though, as Lapoujade insists, the individual for James is directly social, an immediately social reality.

Lapoujade arrives at the social dimension of James's thought along a different path than media and science studies—that of convention. James's emphasis on convention ensures that "it is not individuals that come first, but the signs they exchange." Lapoujade thus underscores how, for James, the relation has ontological priority over the individual: "What is in question, then, is less the individual than the relation that links two individuals."[11] Following James, Lapoujade deploys concepts like individual and social as well as convention, community, and consensus—terms that largely drop out of accounts of the reality of the relational in media and science studies, in favor of concepts like world and network. This is not to say that media and science studies lack a social dimension. On the contrary, the withness that concerns them is as profoundly social as that of convention and community. But the individuals brought into relation are different, as different as their fields of inquiry—neurosciences, algorithms, wireless networks, computational architectures. As such, these studies collectively bring us to a threshold where a new question arises. If James gives ontological priority to the relation and the relational, why does he so often begin with and focus on the individual? Damasio is not wrong to see in James an interest in the making of self and a question about how an individual possesses (and conversely, what the individual is possessed with). What is at stake in the practical and empirical priority James gives to personal experience?

For me, this question goes to the heart of James's philosophy, for his pragmatism and pluralism cannot be understood without considering how his empiricism is related to his broader deployment of "natural diversity" as method. Simply put, the individual in James is foremost a biological individual, and James builds primarily on natural sciences to formulate the individual as a site of "immanent variation" and thus individuation.

This is the line of inquiry I propose as an afterword to Lapoujade's account of James, for it is a line of inquiry that would be impossible to pursue without Lapoujade's careful articulation of what is at stake for James in the establishment of a transcendental field or plane of immanence.

For the most part, my discussion centers on *The Varieties of Religious Experience* for two reasons. First, James's inquiry into religion is notorious for its emphasis on the religious experiences of individuals, or personal religion. Second, *The Varieties of Religious Experience* is something of a turning point in James's philosophy, marking a shift from his earlier work on psychology toward the greater development of pragmatism and radical empiricism in later publications. As such, the work on religious experience allows for a trajectory complementary to Lapoujade's account of radical empiricism and pragmatism, which culminates in a discussion of faith and communities of interpretation. Mine culminates in a discussion of inner dispositions and ecological thinking.

The question of natural diversity concerns the inspiration drawn from biological sciences and especially evolutionary theory on the empirical side of James's philosophy, evident in his tendency to use terms such as "social organism" and "social evolution," and to think in terms of selection, internal variation, and contingency. James does not, however, give ontological priority to the nature of the natural sciences. He works through such sciences to adopt an ontogenetic perspective. His interest lies in ontogeny or ontogenesis rather than ontology *tout court*. Yet, the question of natural diversity raises a thoroughly Jamesian pragmatic question: What is the advantage for us, in our lives, of thinking in terms of natural diversity? At the present moment, when our media and our media studies lead as if inexorably to a restriction of diversity via technological, computational, mathematical or quantic fields of rationality, renewing the question of biological and natural diversity takes on renewed importance, not least because it is in such terms that James arrives at his pragmatic question about the value of spirituality and belief. James's interest in diversity brings us to diversity of all kinds, not only natural diversity but also religious diversity, racial diversity, gender diversity, and even neurodiversity. The broader question, then, is not about the natural per se but about the value of diversity.

Two or More Orders of Logical Inquiry

In *The Varieties of Religious Experience,* James announces at the outset that his subject is "psychological, not religious institutions, but rather religious feelings and religious impulses."[12] To avoid misunderstanding, he continually repeats his intention to center his inquiry on personal religion (rather than institutional religion), because "the inner dispositions of man himself form the center of interest, his conscience, his deserts, his helplessness, his incompleteness."[13] In fact, so willing is he to avoid dispute that, if anyone feels the term religion should refer exclusively to religious institutions, he is willing to use a term other than religion: "Call it conscience or morality, if you yourselves prefer, and not religion—under either name it will be equally worthy of our study."[14] Indeed, the term "conscience," in the etymological sense of both "with-science" and "thorough-knowledge," may describe his goals better than religion, for James aims to show how exceptional states and religious experiences may bring us to a broader, deeper, and higher knowledge that does not contradict science but operates alongside and through it. Conscience, in James's account, happens with and through science.

It is above all in the context of the study of religion that James's methodological emphasis on the individual, in the guise of personal religion, has met with both ire and misunderstanding. Throughout his lectures, James expresses concern that his emphasis on personal religion might prove upsetting to his audience. He worries that some may feel that, if one strips away religious institutions, the resulting account of religion will be purely scientific, anathema to spiritual values. James, then, associates his focus on personal religion with a scientific perspective: "When I handle them biologically and psychologically as if they were mere curious facts of individual history, some of you may think it a degradation of so sublime a subject."[15] It is indeed part of his gambit to look at religious experiences biologically and psychologically, to situate them in the same region as experiential states characterized as psychological disorders.

Ultimately, however, James's goal is not a reductively scientific or naturalistic account of religion. From the outset, he also makes abundantly clear that his inquiry will advance in a two-sided manner.[16] Thus, he introduces two orders of logical inquiry. The first order entails existential judgment, or a proposition about something, with questions that are ontological in bent, such as "what is the nature of it?" and "how did it come about?" The second order involves spiritual judgment, or a proposition of value: "What is the importance, meaning, or significance of it, now that it is here?"[17] Already James is putting his spin on these two orders of logical inquiry. He pursues the first, existential and ontological order via an expanded empiricism (he is not yet using the term radical empiricism). James's survey does, in fact, extend beyond what is normally deemed religious experience, to embrace all manner of exceptional states of perception, including those documented in psychical research.[18] To address the second order of logical inquiry, concerning the judgment of value, he draws on pragmatism, as first articulated by Charles Sanders Peirce.

Once James has set forth these two orders, he issues assurances to those members of his audience who might be apprehensive about a purely empirical inquiry into religion, to the effect that his lectures move purposefully from the first order to the second order, eventually giving pride of place to spiritual values. Indeed, while his discussion continually crosses back and forth between the two orders of inquiry, his account gradually, albeit by fits and starts, alters the proportionate mixture of the two. The scales begin to tip more toward spiritual value and pragmatism roughly midway through the lectures, when he moves from conversion to saintliness: "With this question [what are the practical fruits of religious conversions?] the really important part of our task begins, for you remember that we began all this empirical inquiry not merely to open a curious chapter in the natural history of human consciousness, but rather to attain a spiritual judgment as to the total value and positive meaning of all the religious trouble and happiness which we have seen."[19]

Such remarks may make it seem as if the function of expanded empiricism was merely to make way for pragmatism, as if spontaneously. Such remarks may even give the impression that the empiricism amounts to little more than modern window dressing for the reassertion of perennial religious truths. But the relation between the two orders of logical inquiry is more complex. Once James has established the two orders of inquiry, a third order appears in the offing. As soon as he introduces them, he feels compelled to remind us: "Neither judgment can be deduced immediately from the other. They proceed from diverse intellectual preoccupations, and the mind combines them only by making them first separately, and then adding them together."[20] Put another way, James introduces a disjunctive relation between the empirical and the spiritual orders of his logical inquiry. His twofold inquiry thus turns out to be threefold. What concerns him is not only empiricism and pragmatism, but also the relation between them. Although he does not spell out this third order of judgment as explicitly as the other two, the fact that he claims that the two orders cannot be *deduced* from each other is a clear sign that his judgment here will not proceed deductively. Sprinkled throughout his lectures are indications that he is transforming the procedures of introspection used in *Principles of Psychology* into a method of intuition, reminiscent of that of Henri Bergson.

James is well aware that he is entering Kantian territory with these three orders of judgment, which are like Kant's three syntheses. Not only does James jest that his account might be styled, following Kant, a "Critique of Pure Saintliness," he also proposes in all earnestness a transformation in what counts as knowledge via Kant: "It is not only the Ideas of pure Reason as Kant styled them, that have this power of making us vitally feel presences that we are impotent articulately to describe. All sorts of higher abstractions bring with them the same kind of impalpable appeal."[21] This mutation of Kantian critique is at the heart of James's manner of thinking on the relation between "thatness" (empirical judgment) and "whatness" (spiritual judgment). He writes, "Our faith *that* these unintelligible objects actually exist proves thus to be a full equivalent in *praktischer Hinsicht*, as Kant calls it, from the point of view of our action, for a knowledge of *what* they might be. . . . Everything we know is 'what' it is by sharing in the nature of one of these abstractions."[22]

Such a transformation in the status of knowledge articulated in Kant may be attributed in part to the willingness of the new psychology, both in its Jamesian and Freudian turns, to grapple seriously with nonrational, allegedly pathological states, such as hallucinations, delusions, and dreams. Psychology thus invited a thorough overhaul of Kantian philosophy, one that continues to this day. Deleuze and Guattari, for instance, also challenge Kant's elimination of superstitious beliefs, hallucinations, and fantasies from knowledge in his bid to establish the higher forms of knowledge independently of allegedly pathological forms.[23] Yet, even as they reject Kant's demotion of such realities to psychic reality, they still acknowledge that it was Kant who first posed the question of the productiveness of desire. James's account likewise insists on the reality of religious and psychic experiences and the reality of desire (as satisfaction). What is commonly qualified as psychic reality is not for James lesser than or inferior to what Kant established as higher forms of knowledge. Note, too, that when James speaks of "sharing" in these abstractions, he is introducing the directly social dimension of self in the making. As Damasio underscores, self for James involves a feeling about *what* one possesses (spiritual value and pragmatism). At the same time, what is possessed consists of things and abstractions *that* possess the individual (empiricism).

Teasing out these strands of philosophical engagement woven through James's lectures enables us to look anew at the question of the individual. We now understand James's use of the individual (personal religion) to be a practical, or methodological, point of departure. It is obvious that focusing on the individual, and especially on the individual's mind, gives a good deal of philosophical purchase. Yet James's extensive citations from a variety of sources—clinical, confessional, anecdotal, literary, philosophical, and doctrinal, some anonymous, some renowned—are calculated to loosen the grip of both philosophy in general and philosophy of religion in particular. As such, although my discussion tends to highlight James's philosophy, I must note that at stake for James was not a philosophically restrictive account of the individual but an empirically expansive one.

We can better understand the stakes of his methodological reliance on the individual by turning to the objections raised against it. To Émile Durkheim above all we owe the objection that James's philosophy is a form of individualism that rules out the social or the collective dimension of religious experience, precisely because it does not begin or end with the "collective social fact" embodied in religious institutions.

Pragmatism × Rationalism

Intent as Durkheim was on delineating and consolidating the discipline of sociology, it is not surprising that pragmatism troubled him.[24] Not only does he single out James for criticism at the end of his opus *The Elementary Forms of Religious Life*, published a decade after *Varieties of Religious Experience*, but in the following year (1913), Durkheim devoted a seminar to pragmatism, and it was posthumously published under the title *Pragmatism and Sociology*. Here, too, in the penultimate lecture, his seminar on pragmatism singles out James to contest what Durkheim believes is James's vision of individualism. Durkheim opines, "Intellectual individualism does not imply, as James seems to think, that everyone may arbitrarily believe what he wishes to believe. It simply means that there are separate tasks within the joint enterprise, and that everyone may choose his own in accordance with his temperament."[25]

Note how his characterization of James's notion of belief as arbitrary spurs Durkheim to naturalize the modern hierarchical division of labor: the subordination of individual variation to the "joint enterprise" feels somehow justified. We can understand what leads Durkheim to this stance if we consider what was at stake for him in the context of disciplining sociology: establishing the superiority of rationalism over pragmatism. What particularly disturbs Durkheim about pragmatism is its claim that our formulations of truth do not merely express or copy reality but add something to it. For pragmatism, the rationalist bid for truthful knowledge based on the production (and reproduction) of faithful copies of reality is not so much wrong or unthinkable as it is exceedingly limited. James, for instance, addresses the claims of rationalism in *Varieties of Religious Experience*, namely, that all our beliefs ought ultimately to find for themselves articulate grounds, consisting of four things: definitely stable abstract principles, definite facts of sensation, definite hypotheses based on such facts, and definite inferences logically drawn. He then concludes, "If we look on man's whole mental life as it exists, . . . we have to confess that the part of it of which rationalism can give an account is relatively superficial."[26]

Rationalism is not only empirically narrow in James's opinion, but severely constrained in pragmatic terms as well. Ultimately, the rationalist model of reality and its representation limits the scope of its inquiry to relations obtaining between individual and society by avoiding the pragmatic question: What does the discipline based on faithful copies of reality add to our world that is of advantage, and for whom?

Durkheim believes sociology has the answer to this pragmatic judgment. He thus closes his penultimate lecture on pragmatism and sociology with this response to the ostensible arbitrariness of James's pragmatism: "The fact is that truth, the 'copy' of reality, is not merely redundant or pleonastic. It certainly 'adds' a new world to reality, a world which is more complex than any other. That world is the human and social one. Truth is the means by which a new order of things becomes possible, and that new order is nothing less than *civilization*."[27]

For Durkheim, the truth arrived at through the representation of reality makes for a new world order called civilization whose value is apparently incontestable. Yet it is precisely such fixed values as civilization that James's pragmatism calls into question. At the end of his third lecture on the varieties of religious experience, for instance, James considers the proposal that things like "our Music, our Science, and our so-called 'Civilization,' as these things are now organized and admiringly believed in, form the more genuine religions of our time." His response to such a proposal is scathing: "Certainly the unhesitating and unreasoning way in which we feel that we must inflict our civilization upon 'lower' races, by means of Hotchkiss guns, etc., reminds one of nothing so much as of the early spirit of Islam spreading its religion by the sword."[28]

James, then, does not merely issue a scientific and empirical challenge to the claims of rationalism and its model of reality and representation. For James, rationalism is tantamount to a belief in civilization, which raises the question of what it means to believe in civilization, or in institutions for that matter. Who benefits from such belief? Timothy Mitchell's account of colonial modernity offers a response like that of James. Mitchell shows how the ideological imposition of the rationalist model of reality and representation played a central role in the "civilizing" mission, that is, in imperial conquest and colonial rule.[29] The civilizing mission of museums and world fairs, for instance, deployed a wide range of techniques to impose this model of reality and representation on the geopolitical imagination of the world.[30]

It is here worth evoking Lapoujade's turn to the sociology of Gabriel Tarde. Recall that Durkheim saw Tarde as his principal rival for establishing the new field of sociology. He thus devoted a great deal of energy to discrediting Tarde's approach.[31] Lapoujade does not address this rivalry directly but deftly reveals what is at stake conceptually. He evokes Tarde to steer us away from the binary oppositions that Durkheim's disciplinization of social science tends to encourage—individual versus collective, psychology versus sociology. Lapoujade introduces new concepts that move with, through, and beyond such binary oppositions. Between individual and collective, Lapoujade situates distribution, the distributive field. Between psychology and sociology is intercerebral psychology. For Tarde, an expanded psychology, an intercerebral psychology, promised a sociology with a broader scope of inquiry than the sociology based on the so-called collective social fact of received institutions such as Church and State, a sociology that might address other orders or gradations of the social, such as transportation and communication networks. In sum, instead of the reality and representation model promulgated by Durkheim, James moves us toward a social semiotics attentive to distribution, communication, transportation, and the intercerebral—precisely the techno-psycho-social domain that media studies aims to address today. I return to the possibilities for media studies at the end of this afterword. But to prepare that discussion, I must stick with the facts of James's emphasis on the individual.

Theism × Pluralism

This first excursus through Durkheim's objections to James—the focus on personal religion instead of institutions—gives a sense of what is at stake in James's methodological attention to the individual. Evident now is the expansiveness of James's empiricism in contrast to the restrictiveness of Durkheim's rationalism. Nevertheless, James does not oppose his method of inquiry to that of rationalism. He formulates a contrast. He acknowledges the conceptual purchase afforded by rationalism but finds it too narrow in its investment in the definite—definite principles, definite facts, definite hypotheses, definite inferences.[32] At stake for James, then, is not only the individual as the methodological point of departure. At stake is what *kind* of individual the two philosophies bring into the world. As James's repetition of "definite" to characterize rationalism implies, the bent of empiricism and pragmatism is, in contrast, toward the indefinite. This movement toward the indefinite has consequences for how James delineates his task vis-à-vis the individual.

At one crucial juncture in his study, the lectures on "The Sick Soul," when James feels compelled to differentiate his approach from rationalism in a new register, that of theism, he addresses the problematic of the individual explicitly. This is the contrast he introduces within theism:

> Philosophical theism has always shown a tendency to become pantheistic and monistic, and to consider the world as one unit of absolute fact; and this has been at variance with popular or practical theism, which latter had ever been more or less frankly pluralistic, not to say polytheistic, and shown itself perfectly well satisfied with a universe composed of many original principles, provided we be only allowed to believe that the divine principle remains supreme, and that the others are subordinate.[33]

James feels obligated to introduce such a contrast within theism because his discussion has shifted from the "healthy-minded" to the "sick soul." Unlike the healthy-minded experience, the religious experience of the sick soul is one of direct encounter with evil. Above all, James wishes to avoid transforming the distinction between good and evil into a dialectical relation, in which good overcomes evil through reason, that is, rationalism. He thus takes care to distinguish his method from the dialectical procedures of Hegel, in which the real is the rational, and the movement of reason is one of sublation of unreason. James notes that such a move is only possible because Hegel posits a monistic God as the foundation for the movement of reason. He thus remarks that "on the monistic or pantheistic view, evil, like everything else, must have its foundation in God; and the difficulty is to see how this can possibly be the case if God is absolutely good." Thus, the commitment to rationalism, at least in its Hegelian version, results in difficulty with the question of evil. James concludes, "The monistic philosopher finds himself more or less bound to say, as Hegel said, that everything actual is rational, and that evil, as an element dialectically required, must be pinned in and kept and consecrated and have a function awarded to it in the final system of truth."[34] Indeed, for Hegel, the rational sublation of unreason entails theodicy.

For James, pluralism (and potentially something like polytheism) is the truer tendency. From the perspective of pluralism, evil is not something that can be hemmed in, pinned down, rationally incorporated, dialectically overcome, or otherwise consecrated. It remains irrational, an "alien reality." Oddly enough, even though James is supposedly dealing with the sick soul in this context, he associates pluralism with healthy-mindedness. If this association appears odd, it is because James has already established that the sick soul, which undergoes an experience of evil, is essential to religious experience. Clearly, however, James does not wish to advance a binary opposition or contradictory relation between the healthy-minded and the sickly souled, or between good and evil, which would allow for a dialectical overcoming, not only of evil but also of the sick soul. In other words, he aims to stick to this idea: what are deemed to be pathological states are not simply states to be overcome through the progress of reason. In effect, he is calling on the science of psychology to impede the march of reason and progress, of civilization. He is calling for another science, another kind of reason, and another way of thinking progressively, which does not demand a rational whole. He puts it this way: "Here we have the interesting notion fairly and squarely presented to us, of there being elements of the universe which may make no rational whole in conjunction with the other elements, and which, from the point of view of any system which those other elements make up, can only be considered so much irrelevance and accident—so much 'dirt,' as it were, and matter out of place."[35]

In sum, James's goal is to keep the "matter out of place" in play conceptually and ethically, to say yes to irrelevance and accident. For instance, to use a contemporary example, the accidents that make for neurodiversity can neither be consecrated nor overcome by the advance of reason. Nor can they be relegated to the status of happy accidents.

The Indefinite Aggregate Individual

These instances of James's procedural use of contrast bring us to a fuller understanding of what kind of individual is at stake. The individual for James is not the strictly rational individual. Nor is it the individual of absolute idealism (the self-making, self-perfecting human). When he expresses his discontent with "every form of philosophy in which the world appears as one flawless unit of fact," he immediately adds, "Such a unit is an *Individual*, and in it the worst parts must be as essential as the best, must be as necessary to make the individual what he is; since if any part whatever in an individual were to vanish or alter, it would no longer be *that* individual at all."[36] In this way, he contests both rationalism and idealism while building on them.

If we build on James's remarks on the individual in the context of his resistance to rationalism and absolute idealism, the individual for James might best be described as a plane of consistency or composition whose unity is virtual. When he speaks of pluralism, for instance, he evokes "a universe composed of many original principles," and the aim of his pluralism is to stick with the fact of heterogeneity in religious experience. Personal religious experience, then, is experience composed of many original heterogeneous principles, some of them irrelevant and accidental from the perspective of reason. The individual comes into being through a nonrational process of indefinite composition. For James, then, the rational, definite individual of individualism is but a constriction of this larger nonrational and indefinite individual.

James strives to convey something of this plane of composition in the very process of composing his lectures. At numerous junctures, he signals his concern that his manner of presentation is introducing too much definiteness across his examples. In fact, the way in which he composes his lectures entails an avoidance of strategies of both individualization and generalization: although he works from personal accounts, not only is his selection heterogenous in terms of its range of anonymous and famous personalities and religions (it is as eccentric and eclectic as the personalities that populate it), but his reading practice also works at the level of variation within and across individuals. It is not a stretch to read these lectures as a literary sort of "intercerebral composition." The model for James's treatment of the human individual as a plane of composition might be said to be like a book composed of a series of lectures or essays. The human is a work in progress, everlasting only through prolonging its indefiniteness, indefinitely.

But I wish here to return to my guiding question, about James's use of the individual, and here I mean the human individual, as a methodological point of departure. Much as it is appealing and fitting to characterize James's discussion of the individual as performative or compositional, there is a risk of inadvertently positing isomorphism across gradations of reality—human, book, world, universe. He continually warns against the tendency of philosophy toward isomorphism, that is, toward imposing the same paradigm of the individual on different orders of reality— on the human individual, the social, the world, the universe. The result would be a cosmology to which James objects, for empirical, pragmatic, and pluralist reasons. Thus, I propose to turn to the biological stance implicit in James's method of the individual, evident in his references to evolution and his recourse to terms related to natural sciences, such as "function," "vital," "animal," and "satisfaction," in the hope that greater attention to his empiricism will reveal something more of its relation to pragmatism.

Surely it did not escape notice that when James brings forth the indefinite and "aggregate" individual and the idea of composing with many original principles, he also introduces the notion of subordination. The individual-in-the-making entails both coordination and subordination. Again James will turn to the natural sciences to formulate his account of coordination and subordination empirically, in biological and vital terms. Later I consider how his turn to coordination and subordination allows him to avoid a homogeneous plane of composition and a thoroughly flat ontology. But first, let's consider how nature as "dirt," not as ground, interests him.

Material Flows and Evolutionary Theory

At key junctures, Lapoujade highlights how James's empiricism contests hylomorphism, that is, the assumption that form has de facto superiority over matter. Let me reiterate his basic argument. For James, the attempts of Kant and Husserl to establish a transcendental field fall short because they do not go beyond received psychological forms. Even though these transcendental philosophies reject the empiricism and naturalism of psychology and strive to strip it away to get at its pure forms, the result is merely a stripped-down version of the forms already given by psychology. James reminds us, however, that the empiricism and naturalism of psychology are not the basic problem. The problem is that psychology does not know how to pursue material flows and thus makes poor distinctions and extracts bad forms. James may be said to give de facto priority to material flows, which allows him to establish a transcendental field autonomous of psychology, autonomous of its forms and thus of hylomorphic schemata.

James's inspiration for tracking material flows is the natural sciences. Lapoujade gives two examples in passing that confirm as much. At one point, Lapoujade evokes the formation of salt crystals, arguing that the sodium and chloride are as much a part of the experiment or experience of crystallization as the human experimenter. Experience, like scientific experimentation, applies equally to "subjects" and "objects," which strictly speaking do not exist at this level. At another juncture, when speaking of "unities of consistency," Lapoujade uses the example of a plant to describe how James envisions the way in which parts hang together: light is held together by the photosynthesis of plants, and conversely, plants are held together by light. He concludes, "All transcendence is rejected since the parts are no longer unified by a superior rationality—an exterior point of view; they hold each other together."[37] We can better understand the usefulness of the individual as a point of departure for James's philosophical establishment of a transcendental field if we more closely attend to how he tracks the material flows revealed through the experimental vantage of the natural sciences, especially concerning evolution.

James's approach recalls the natural sciences in that its individual, the organism, implies a unity of functions, not of forms. It builds on theories of natural evolution in which the individual is the site of variation. Indeed, when James speaks of varieties of religious experience, we might take the term "varieties" in its biological sense: novelty does not arise at the level of species or of genera. Novelty arises through variations introduced by chance through the individual organism. In effect, the individual is a sort of pivot or relay, or even a buffer zone: chance variations move through the organism to affect populations. The source of those variations, because they occur by chance or at random, is difficult to pin down; they may arise from within the organism, or they may be triggered by external changes in the environment, or both. There is a world of difference, then, between a science based on varieties (James) and a science laying claim to elementary forms (Durkheim). Elementary forms imply some sort of universal geometry, authoritative laws underlying and determining all variations, and rational unity in the form of civilization is the end game. Varieties imply material flows in relation to functions and unities of consistency, that is, ecologies, which are moving toward diversity.

Put another way, elementary forms tend toward what is often called social Darwinism, in which some organisms are deemed to be higher, more advanced, or more civilized forms of life than others, for evolution (survival of the fittest) is construed in terms of optimization, which is associated with "higher" functions of reason. Although Darwin himself occasionally flirted with social Darwinism, his theory of evolution is today considered, on the whole, to eschew a hierarchy of species or of varieties within species. Survival of the fittest is best construed in terms of satisfying rather than optimizing.[38] Which is to say, organisms cross the threshold of survival if they satisfy certain criteria. They need not optimize. As such, their unity of consistency may include all manner of jury-rigged, superfluous, or even ill-fashioned functions, provided the whole satisfies the criteria for survival. There are, then, two lines of thinking descended from Darwin—Darwinism and social Darwinism. The former is what we think of as contemporary evolutionary theory.

James's philosophy runs resolutely counter to social Darwinism. He takes up evolutionary theory in a manner that is more in agreement with contemporary evolutionary theory than with the social Darwinism widely advanced in his day, made popular especially through the work of Herbert Spencer. The goal of pluralism, diversity, is imagined not in terms of optimizing diversity, but rather in terms of satisfying. To optimize diversity would be to crush it. For the same reason, James does not strive to eliminate the concerns of his rivals. James incessantly strives for a vaster field in which something like Durkheim's civilization need not be rejected outright, for it may aid the goals of pluralism. James merely submits that civilization is never something to optimize. European civilization is not a form to impose on the so-called lower races, in a hylomorphic manner, even if, as he says, "It seems the natural thing for us to listen whilst the Europeans talk."[39]

Regions × Representations

Already it is clear that the natural sciences of biology and evolution afford James a way to track materials flows and functions instead of purifying already existing forms. They offer a way to establish a transcendental field, which allows him to extend the empirical lessons of the natural sciences into his account of history and society. That is *what* is at stake in the precedence given to personal religion in *Varieties of Religious Experience*. Personal religion is the gateway into psychological variations arising within the biological individual. The individual is the site of variants for selection and thus for social evolution. James thus comes to challenge the idea that social evolution takes place only (or primarily) through a heroic figure who battles for the survival of the nation or "race." It also occurs through the saintly demon who acknowledges and cultivates her involuntary variations. The biological and psychological individual is more like a social threshold, for it functions both as a pivot and buffer zone vis-à-vis sociohistorical transformation or evolution. As such, James's guiding question is essentially that of what a threshold can do: What is the agency of a threshold? What does acting as a threshold bring into the world?

Let me turn to what initially feels like a simple figure of speech for James in his assessment of religious experience, a riff on Matthew 7:16: "By their fruits ye shall know them, not by their roots."[40]

James's alteration of the passage from Matthew is noteworthy. In keeping with received interpretations of Matthew, James submits that appearances of virtue are not proofs of grace. But then he adds, "The *roots* of a man's virtue are inaccessible to us."[41] Such a claim may appear odd for the philosopher who would soon call his empiricism *radical*, pertaining to the roots. Why not call it fruitful empiricism? In fact, James is countering Matthew's certainty that figs do not grow on thistles, or grapes from thorns. James leaves open the possibility that something fig-like in nutritive value may grow from something thistle-like in appearance. Conceptually speaking, he takes up Matthew's valorization of the fruits only to introduce indeterminacy between root and fruit. Conversely, when his empiricism goes radical and addresses the roots, it is from the perspective of its fruits (pragmatism), but without assuming any correlation between roots and fruits in the manner of classical empiricism or rationalism. Root and fruit, empiricism and pragmatism, are in a relation of inclusive disjunction. They do not resemble each other. The one does not represent the other.

The task of radical empiricism is to find a way to acknowledge the reality, the real effects, of those inaccessible roots, which lie below the ground, without recourse to classical empiricism (correspondence) or rationalism (representation). Note that the ground does not serve as a foundation; it does not ground anything. On the contrary, thinking in terms of the ground is what makes roots seem inaccessible. Radical empiricism might thus be characterized as a process of excavation. Radical empiricism digs beneath the received forms that appear to be foundational, to be the ground. What is unearthed is an aggregate of roots and dirt. Thus, James writes, "If you tear out one, its roots bring out more with them . . . whatever is real is telescoped and diffused into other reals," a statement for which Lapoujade provides the perfect gloss: "Each thing that we attempt to pry loose bears with it a halo of connections, its region."[42]

James's empiricism might be characterized by the way in which it deals with this plant, this biological individual—it has roots and fruits, but we cannot access its roots through the forms of correspondence proposed in classical empiricism. Nor can we claim that the fruits represent the roots in the manner of rationalism, treating the ground as the foundation for representation. Expanded or radical empiricism deals with the region, the interconnected stuff of dirt and roots. If we here think of potatoes or peanuts rather than plants with fruits above ground, we come closer still to James's vision of the individual organism and of the psyche: a mass of dirt with fruity nodes and root network. Like Freud, James is interested in "dirty" regions. Like Freud, he finds that such commonly "inaccessible" zones are where everything is happening. But they are only dirty by convention, and James suggests that the dirt-laced region is also a halo of connections, saintly. In sum, this halo-like dirt-riven region is where we grasp the whole of the individual, as a network and patchwork aggregate of flows and functions.

A contrast with Durkheim is again useful for understanding James's wager on the empirical perspective afforded by the natural sciences. In the conclusion to *The Elementary Forms of Religious Life*, Durkheim expresses both his agreement and his differences with James: "This entire study rests on the postulate that the unanimous feeling of believers down the ages cannot be mere illusion. Therefore, like a recent apologist of faith [James],

I accept that religious belief rests on a definite experience, whose demonstrative value is, in a sense, not inferior to that of scientific experiments, though it is different."[43]

It is worth noting how thoroughly Durkheim misrepresents James, even in these apparently descriptive statements. First, James does not postulate the unanimity of belief. On the contrary, when James works through the unanimity that emerges when one reads the "classic tradition" of writing on mystical experiences, he does so only to add that such unanimity is only possible by eliminating the more diabolical side of mystical experience that is ruled out as insanity.[44] Diversity is the aim of his study, not unanimity. Second, for James, religious belief rests on indefinite experience, not a definite experience. Finally, if forced to rank science and religion, James would detect a false abstraction, a false hierarchy. For James, religious experience is not inferior or superior to science; it is higher, deeper, and vaster, and as such, it pushes the boundaries of what the sciences take seriously. Ultimately, James is not interested in separating and hierarchizing religion and science. It is the potentially anarchic withness of science and religion that is of interest to James. Again, conscience, literally con-science, aptly describes his take on the relation of religion to science. Even in Durkheim's brief characterization of James, he merely announces his own commitment to unanimity (not diversity), the definitive (not indeterminacy), and hierarchy (not heterogeneity).

The contrast becomes starker when Durkheim picks up James's figure of the tree. He writes, "I too think 'that a tree is known by its fruits,' and that its fertility is the best proof of what its roots are worth. But merely because there exists 'a religious experience,' if you will, that is grounded in some manner (is there, by the way, any experience that is not?), it by no means follows that the reality which grounds it should conform objectively with the idea that believers have of it."[45] Note how Durkheim eliminates not only consideration of the dirt but also of the roots. An abstract form—the ground—is introduced between root and fruit, which allows for the fruit to appear to represent the value of the roots. He proposes that the reality of the roots is known only through its representation (the fruits). For Durkheim, the organic relation between roots and fruits justifies the rationalist model of representation. While it is true that fruits are in relation to roots, Durkheim mistakenly presents their relation as unidirectional and univocal, as rational and representational: it is as if the fruits follow rationally from roots, and as such, provide a rational accounting of their worth. At stake for Durkheim, then, is transforming Matthew's figure of the tree into a relation between reality and its representation. To do so, he must introduce an abstract form (the ground) to drive a wedge between reality (roots) and representation (fruits); rationalism may then enter to provide an evaluation, as if neutrally.

In this way, rationalism preemptively narrows the field of inquiry: through its reliance on received abstract forms. Rationalism can only hear reason. As such, in Durkheim's account, because believers do not provide an objective or rational understanding of the grounds for their religious life, we cannot rely on their words. For him, belief is fundamentally misrepresentation and, as such, is in need of demystification by the social scientist. Durkheim thus adds, "The very fact that the way in which this reality has been conceived has varied infinitely in different times is enough to prove that none of these conceptions expresses it adequately."[46]

For Durkheim the social scientist, variation is a sign of diversity, and diversity is a sign of inadequacy. His drive toward adequacy leads him to strip away variation and diversity, hence the method of paring religious life down to its elementary forms. The ground of sociology, then, is not composed of anything (such as dirt and roots, or regions, nodes, and networks). The ground is supposed to be an objective foundation that grounds the rationality of the elementary forms obtained through disciplinary reduction.

Such a method ultimately fails to establish a transcendental field autonomous of received forms of psychology. It strips away the diverse realities of religious experience to arrive at purified versions of the forms already established in psychology. Indeed, Durkheim's take on psychology has been described as "more or less the classical paradigm of conditioned response."[47] The social scientist assumes the de facto superiority of forms over material flows, which is extended into a hierarchy of forms (civilized forms over primitive forms, for instance). When social science fails to construct an autonomous transcendental field for sociology, it not only falls back on elementary forms already given in psychology, but also endorses received ideas about the natural hierarchy of things. The "social fact," then, is merely the received psychosocial form of modern reason, which is allowed to encompass and permeate everything, while variation, transformation, and diversity become unthinkable. Everything begins with the imposition of form onto matter, or the rationalization of material flows. It is in this way that civilization, as the rationalization of materials flows (including flows of people), comes to function as an incontestable value for Durkheim.

The hylomorphic schema implicit in the establishment of elementary (rational) forms of religion invites a paradigm of environmental determinism and a rejection of ecology (complex of dirt, roots, fruits). Thus, Durkheim always wants to place the organism unambiguously in its environment, to understand it in terms of its environment, and likewise with the mind: "Just as our physical organism gets it nourishment outside itself, so our mental organism feeds itself on ideas, sentiments, and practices that come to us from society."[48]

In contrast, James begins with a twofold approach: "To understand a thing rightly we need to see it both out of its environment and in it, and to have acquaintance with the whole range of its variations."[49] The first step, of isolating a thing, however, does not reduce it to elementary forms. Isolating a thing allows for closer scrutiny, whence James's delight in the microscope: "We learn most about a thing under a microscope, in its most exaggerated form."[50] In other words, when James suggests looking at a thing outside its environment, the aim is not purification in the sense of stripping away variations. On the contrary, the close view adds complexity. The halo of connections, the dirty stuff, will cling to the roots. The individual under the microscope reveals a complex aggregate of functions related to material flows. The second step, considering the thing in its environment, takes these materials flows into account, puts them in relation. Such flows signal a connectivity with the environment which cannot be reduced to paradigms of grounding, encompassing, or permeating, that is, environmental determinism. For instance, when James proposes to place the saint back in her environment and estimate her total function, he finds not only that the saint is not infallible, but that the saint may also be considered ill adapted to her environment.[51] This is where empiricism segues into pragmatism, for we confront the consequences of our criteria: "How is success to be absolutely measured when there are so many environments and so many ways of looking at the adaptation? It cannot be measured absolutely; the verdict will vary according to the point of view adopted."[52]

Here, too, James does not dismiss rationalism. Instead he situates the claims of reason within regions, zones, or environments in a manner that recalls Michel Foucault's delineation of "fields of rationality," which followed from Foucault's similar bid to avoid a massive modernity thesis based on Rationalization writ large.[53] James then reminds us that each dirty region with its halo of connections also implies a perspective with distinct criteria for judgment—a subjectivity.

Oddly enough, although he consistently takes care to link the subjective to the objective (field of rationality), James's approach has often been characterized as thoroughly, even excessively subjective. This is surely because James relies heavily on facts related to psychology. Even when he draws on natural sciences, he tends to align those facts with the facts of psychology. But there is a reason for this methodological tendency. Above all, James wishes to avoid explanations of experience that lay claim to objectivity based on accounts of external determinants. Here, too, James turns to the natural sciences to rethink the objective side of subjectivity.

Immanent Variation

In the form of evolutionary theory sometimes called adaptationism, changes in the environment are said to drive evolution, and organisms fight tooth and claw with one another to be the first to adapt to, and thus to succeed in, the altered environment. Adaptationism stresses the Malthusian component of evolutionary theory and reinforces the social Darwinism that James rejects. Adaptationism situates the agency of organisms in a double bind: organisms are highly active in their struggle for survival yet primarily passive or reactive in relation to their environment. They are not generative or creative. Such a view of evolution tends to yoke competition with optimization, and even to conflate them, as if unfettered competition would produce optimal outcomes. In contrast, as James's study of religious experience attests, he makes room for mal- or ill-adaptation. The saint is one who appears poorly adapted to the exigencies associated with sociopolitical formations based on warfare and competition. The saint is at odds with institutional religions with their doctrines and dogma. If James calls attention to maladaptation in the context of social evolution, it is to place greater emphasis on "internal variation," that is, variations that arise within individual organisms to affect populations.

James likewise places the emphasis on personal experience and inwardness in his account of religious experience, because he wishes to establish his distance from evolutionary theories based on external pressures, competition, and optimization. The poorly adapted organism is generative, proposing an alteration whose value can only be gauged in terms of how it is prolonged socially and historically. Strictly speaking, then, the variation that arises within the individual is not internal in the sense of contained within it. It is immanent variation.

His emphasis on immanent variation encourages me to characterize James's thought as ecological. He is interested not only in how environments alter organisms, but also (and principally) in how organisms alter themselves and their environment, creating zones and regions that become existential ecologies. Here, too, his critique of unwarranted reliance on foundations—the ground—is in evidence. The external environment is not the ground for ecological thinking. Nor is the ground adaptation. Beneath the apparent ground of adaptation (the adaptation of organisms to their environment) is the movement of variation and selection, which allows for a wide range of weird adaptations and generates so many environments. Evolution need not optimize. It need only satisfy.

When James draws on natural sciences to look at social evolution in terms of immanent variation, he frequently refers to a perspective that is at once higher, deeper, and vaster. Initially, such terminology may appear contradictory. How can a perspective be at once higher, deeper, and vaster? The answer lies in the transcendental field, or as Lapoujade styles it by reference to Deleuze, the plane of immanence. As a field or plane, James's vantage is vast. It is also deep because it tracks what is ontologically prior and empirically deeper than ordinary appearance, and which does not resemble its expression. Yet this vast and deep underlying plane is not flat. It is a field, coursing with energies and material flows, charged with functions—thinkable via Riemannian topology, fluid dynamics, or even quantum mechanics. Such a plane is not that of geometry; it is like a diagrammatic plan. As such, it may afford higher views that do not transcend the field—instances of localized transcendence.

Localized transcendence on a plane of immanence, in contrast to a transcendent point of view, implicates "us," body and soul. Although the plane of pure experience is autonomous of received psychological forms, it cannot be approached or described independently of our concrete lived experience. James does not intend his transcendental field to pose some sort of abstract, quasi-scientist solution to the modern crisis of knowledge—the crisis of groundlessness, the abyss. On the contrary, the ongoing appeal and challenge of James's development of a plane of pure experience comes of its engagement with *lived abstractions*—with concrete planes of consistency or composition. Lived abstractions are at once subjectivities and ecologies. If James constantly refers to the inner, to inwardness, to personal religion and individual experience, it is his method of getting at immanence concretely.

Individuation

Individual experience in James might best be characterized in terms of a holding pattern within an ongoing process of creative individuation (immanent variation). Indeed, his treatment of the individual shows great affinity with Gilbert Simondon's philosophy of individuation. The affinity is especially evident when James evokes the processes of crystallization and magnetization to develop an energetic model of the psyche. At one point, for instance, James writes, "The temperament . . . is like a water of crystallization in which the individual's character is set."[54] Initially, such a statement may seem loosely figurative or diffusely metaphoric. Yet the consistency of his usage of a range of terms and concepts associated with energetic systems, such as equilibrium, phase, center of energy, polarization, oscillation, and field, suggests a highly coherent vision. Such terms are part of an effort to delineate a consistent account of the processes of individuation involved in concrete, lived changes in subjective state.

If we build on Simondon's account of the process of crystallization, which is integral to his philosophy of individuation, we may arrive at a fuller understanding of what is at stake for James. Simondon begins with the metastable state of the supersaturated solution, which "harbors potentials that are incompatible because they belong to heterogeneous dimensions of being."[55] Only when the metastable state dephases does it take on structure, spurring the formation of crystals. Thus, a small impurity introduced into a supersaturated solution triggers the formation of crystals. The result is a crystalline form or structure surrounded by its water of crystallization. Because some water of crystallization is also retained within the crystalline lattice, Simondon invites us to think initially in terms of an "internal milieu" and an "external milieu." If the crystal is removed from its external milieu, it ceases to grow. If left in the water, the crystal may continue to grow, or, depending on how the system oscillates, it may shrink. In other words, the two milieus, internal and external, affect each other and affect the crystal as well. They might be said to communicate, but their communication would be best characterized as affective, relational. To address this relation, Simondon introduces the notion of an "associated milieu" that arises across the external and internal milieus. The external milieu, then, is not the ground for crystallization; it does not determine the process. Nor does the internal milieu. These milieus retain something of the potentiality of the original metastable state. As such, they entail a high degree of indeterminacy. Simondon uses the term "preindividual" to characterize this reserve of potentiality that sustains indeterminacy in the system. If anything can be said to determine the process, it is the associated milieu, as it stretches across external and internal milieus, putting them in relation.

The associated milieu, however, faces in two directions. On the one hand, it carries preindividual being within it. It implies inwardness, an inward orientation, a sort of possession that makes for self, to evoke another of James's concepts. It is more like a direction (orientated toward the internal milieu) rather than a location (within the internal milieu). On the other hand, the associated milieu also runs across the internal and external milieus, and Simondon uses the term "transindividual" to refer to this kind of relation, which is, in effect, a determining force of distribution passing through the newly dephased state or a phase that comprises an individual and its environment.

When James tells us that the individual's character is set within its water of crystallization, he invites us to think in terms of an external milieu (temperament) surrounding some kind of form or structure (character). James generally uses the term "margin" to refer to the external milieu. Like Simondon, he is not content with the idea of an inert or deterministic external milieu, which might be mistaken for the ground. Consequently, to explain the force of the margin, James turns to the idea of a field, drawing on the paradigm of magnetic forces: "The important fact which this 'field' formula commemorates is the indetermination of the margin."[56] Like the associated milieu for Simondon, which inwardly retains the residual potentiality of the metastable system (preindividual being), the notion of margin-field for James introduces indeterminacy into the system. He thus assures that the center is not construed as an inert structure or immutable form. Character takes on an energetic function. It implies a center of energy. James thus adds, "It lies around us like a 'magnetic field' inside of which our center of energy turns like a compass-needle, as the present phase of consciousness alters into its successor."[57]

The evocation of the magnetic field of the compass provides insight into James's turn to the logic of direction to move beyond the narrow confines of representation. Lapoujade repeatedly brings this directional bent of James's thought to the fore: "The idea has the particular property of directing our thought in a specific direction. Ideas are guides." He also notes, "James's philosophy is not foremost a philosophy of knowledge. As we have seen, the idea is not a representation but that which promotes acting in a determined direction."[58] Yet, James situates direction within an energetic system, on a magnetized field. A direction only emerges in relation a polarized field, on which the orientation of the compass needle toward the north, for instance, offers a "little absolute" for the reckoning of travel in all directions. As Lapoujade remarks, "to be pluralist consists of allowing relations to be laid out in all directions."[59]

Thinking of the psyche in terms of a polarized field pointing (potentially) in all directions allows James to address various personalities, types, and characters—what he also calls the "personal center of energy," or more felicitously, "inner equilibrium."[60] The center and the margin of the psyche are in a polarized and thus energized relation, which James describes in terms of expansion and contraction of the personal field. He paves the way for his field concept by noting, "Usually when we have a wide field we rejoice, for we then see masses of truth together. . . . At other times, of drowsiness, illness, or fatigue, our fields may narrow almost to a point, and we find ourselves correspondingly oppressed and contracted."[61] The expansion and contraction of our personal fields is akin to the growing and shrinking of the crystal set within its water of crystallization. Like the crystal, our character is not in control of its expansion and contraction. "There is a push, an urgency, within our very experience, against which we are on the whole powerless, and which drives us in a direction that is the destiny of our belief."[62] There is something nonconscious within the system, a reserve of potentiality that builds indeterminacy into the system.

Steven Meyer provides a fine summary of this movement in James's thought toward nonconsciousness:

An impressive range of experiences—dreams, hypnotism, automatisms, hysteria, multiple personality, demoniacal possession, witchcraft, manias, and genius like—seemed to testify to the existence of states of mind that were exceptions to the general rule that a mental state, in order to exist, had to be conscious. Common to them all was the subject's apparent loss of control over his or her own actions and failure to know why something was being done or even that it was happening at all.[63]

While the indeterminacy cannot be definitely located, it implies a directional sort of inwardness that is not reducible to form (character or crystal). Nor is it reducible to the external or internal milieus. Variation is immanent. James does not, then, replace a deterministic environment with an indeterminate one. Like Simondon, he is interested in the constraints (internal limits) on the system that make for its conditions, which put the structure (character's center of energy) into relation with its environment (margin). This is where Simondon introduces "transindividual" in his account of crystallization. The transindividual relation arises across the crystal and its milieu, or more precisely across the crystal, its internal milieu, and its external milieu. It at once keeps the system open to all directions and imparts a direction to individuation. Similarly, James introduces the "transmarginal region," which "contains every kind of matter."[64] Like the dirty stuff evoked previously, it implies a plurality of actual connections in which the thing is enmeshed.

In this way, James's account of individual character opens into psychic individuation. Our personal character initially appears to be all there is to the psychological individual. But it turns out to have a center of energy, or inner equilibrium. The individual arises on a polarized field, arriving at some kind of equilibrium, which produces a center and a margin, an energized center and a potentialized milieu. James thus evokes "change of equilibrium . . . movement of new psychic energies toward the personal center and recession of old ones toward the margins" and "shiftings of inner equilibrium, those changes of the personal center of energy."[65] The inner equilibrium is not, however, a simple or classical equilibrium. It is not an oscillating system that will eventually settle on a stable mixture or balance of forces. Inner equilibrium entails equilibrium away from (classical) equilibrium. It is ever in movement, unstable, unfixed. Its energies continually expand or contract, advance or recede. James's notion of inner equilibrium thus recalls the preindividual being of Simondon's account, which is potentially held in reserve, not yet activated. As such, it makes for a kind of inner limit on the system, a constraint on the direction of phasing and dephasing. Yes, it can dephase in any direction, but now it is prolonging its dephasing in this direction, phasing in this way. *That* (empirically) is *what* (pragmatically) it is doing, where it is going. This is a philosophy of individuation as immanent variation.

Machinic Thought

True to the empiricist impulse—"the empiricist is constrained to an incessant building of bridges, in every direction," as Lapoujade puts it in chapter 2, James is compelled to consider diverse pathways, that is, variation and diversity among individuals. James thus notes, "Different individuals present constitutional differences in this matter of width of field."[66] The energetic model of individuation allows him to clear the ground to establish a transcendental field (the plane of immanence he calls pure experience) for considering various individual or personal experiences. Yet the aim of the energetic model is not merely empirical accuracy. James's goal is not merely to ensure consistency with the natural sciences. The natural sciences provide James a way to move beyond forms and structures, toward a focus on flows and functions, phases and fields.

This move is also calculated to avoid the simplistic rationalism of the social sciences, whereby received psychological forms are retained to impose the values of modern Western civilization. Where the social sciences introduce an opposition between individual and society while subordinating the individual to the social fact, the natural sciences allow for an inverse procedure. The natural sciences allow us to see the individual as a site of variation. Yet, as James is aware, the natural sciences thus run the risk of instating the individual as a site for disciplinary forms of knowledge (psychiatry, clinic sciences, genetics)—in the form of what James calls "medical materialism," for instance.[67] The pragmatic question must intervene. What is the value of looking at personal experience from the angle of the transcendental field of pure experience? What is the value of taking the biological individual into account, adopting the stance of individuation (natural diversity and the energetic model) afforded by the natural sciences?

When his focus is on the healthy-minded and able-bodied individual at the center of modern society, James does not hesitate to consider its functioning in terms of the engine: "Every individual soul, in short, like every individual machine or organism, has its own best conditions of efficiency. A given machine will run best under a certain steam-pressure, a certain amperage; an organism under a certain diet, weight, or exercise."[68] James does not side with this clinical vision of machinic optimization, but neither does he reject the image of the organism as a machine. In other words, James does not endorse the critical stance claiming that modernity is transforming organisms into mechanisms, natural phenomena into machines. The problem is not mechanization as such. If modern societies can mechanize us, it is because there is already something mechanistic to us, body and soul. Our bodies are engine-like; our minds are engine-like. They entail matter-energy flows that become organized or structured around an ongoing dephasing through phasing, an equilibrium away from equilibrium.

Two interrelated lines of inquiry thus become necessary when we address the problem of modern mechanization. First, there is the path pursued by Simondon, who deploys the philosophy of individuation to turn the question around. If humans can be mechanized, he submits, it is not only because our bodies and minds are already somehow machinic, but also because our technologies, our machines, are increasingly organism-like. For Simondon, this new perspective on technologies—understanding them in terms of their individuation—invites an overhaul of terminology. Thus, he writes of technical individuals and modes of existence that are akin to natural individuals and modes of existence. But, in keeping with the relational view availed by the transcendental field, the living individual and technical individual do not resemble each other. Theirs is a relation of semblance.[69] James of course does not pursue the question of technology as rigorously as does Simondon, yet James's philosophy implies a similar process of deflating technophobic discourses on mechanization (not because he likes mechanization, but because technophobia tends to obscure rather than shed light on the exercise of power), while explicitly undermining the ontological divide so often posited between mechanism and organism (the psyche is like an engine). If our souls are becoming more engine-like, our machines are becoming more mindful, soulful. How do we account for this semblance?

The second line of inquiry begins by contesting the bias toward the smooth functioning of machines. When James says that the soul, like the machine, has its own best conditions of efficiency, he is considering the soul in terms of what passes for healthy functioning, from the perspective of healthy-minded science. But the overall trajectory of his account of religious experience is based on what are usually deemed pathological or exceptional states. The sick soul, he insists, will tell us more about the value of religious experience than healthy-mindedness will. His approach to the psyche here meshes with that of Deleuze and Guattari, who propose machines whose functioning depends on always breaking down: "In desiring-machines everything functions at the same time, but amid hiatuses and ruptures, breakdowns and failures, stalling and short circuits, distances and fragmentations, within a sum that never succeeds in bringing its various parts together so as to form a whole."[70]

For James, then, the modern "problem of science and technology" stems from procedures dedicated solely to the optimization of the internal equilibrium of machines and psyches. Such optimization entails a drive for efficiency instead of sufficiency. It places optimization over and above satisfaction. Optimization is not even capable of considering satisfaction; it does not take our psychic or existential well-being into account. But how are we to get from optimization to satisfaction?

The Mind-Cure Movement

Those "monstrous aberrations of nature," saints, may show us the way, not as ideals or paragons, but as monsters and aberrations. If James characterizes his account as a critique of pure saintliness, it is because his goal is not saintliness as such, but satisfaction.[71] Satisfaction will depend on arriving at social practices affording a twofold movement of individuation. On the one hand, it will be a matter of maximizing relations to preindividual, or "prepersonal," reserves of being, that is, expanding psychic diversity by bringing marginalized experiences to the fore. On the other hand, it will involve minimizing procedures of optimization, which amounts to relativizing individualism and individualization, pushing each into the margins as one possibility among others. Thus, James goes to great lengths to avoid turning the contrast between the healthy-minded (once-born) and the sick soul (twice-born) into categories. He rejects a binary opposition between them, or a simple choice for one over the other. He positions them instead as tendencies on a polarized, charged field. Both tendencies may then be empirically tracked to their "inner" pragmatic limits. This is why James devotes so much attention to the mind-cure movement. If he is to avoid shoring up the dualist stances and binary oppositions that too often crop up in the study of religion, his critique has to explore the polarization of experience, to consider the consequences in both directions— the healthy mind and the sick soul.

The mind-cure movement that gathered steam in the 1890s pushed for alternative, or complementary, medical practices, with an emphasis on the importance of emotional and mental states in sickness and healing— mental healing. It championed practices similar to today's biofeedback, visualization, meditation, and so forth.[72] James strongly defended the mind-cure movement, arguing against legislation that threatened to undermine these "irregular" healers.[73] In *Varieties of Religious Experience*, he deals with this movement at length to consider what healthy-mindedness has to offer. The mind-cure movement reveals for him the inner limit of healthy-mindedness, both its potential and its constraints.

James characterizes healthy-mindedness thus: "In its involuntary version, healthy-mindedness is a way of feeling happy about things immediately. In its systematic variety, it is an abstract way of conceiving things as good."[74] What disturbs him about such healthy-mindedness, especially in its systematic variety, is its tendency to remove all that is not deemed happiness from the realm of well-being. He remarks that "like every emotional state, happiness has blindness and insensibility to opposing facts, self-protection against disturbance."[75] As such, when happiness takes on a systematic mindset, the result is a systematized blindness and insensibility—which James associates not only with medical materialism but also with "evolutionism." He offers this explanation of evolutionism:

> In that "theory of evolution," which, gathering momentum for a century, has within the past twenty-five years swept so rapidly over Europe and America, we see the ground laid for a new sort of religion of Nature, which has entirely displaced Christianity from the thought of a large part of our generation. The idea of universal evolution lends itself to a doctrine of general meliorism, which fits the religious needs of the healthy-minded so well that it seems almost as if it might have been created for their use. Accordingly we find "evolutionism" interpreted thus optimistically and embraced as a substitute for the religion they were born in.[76]

Here, too, James is not dismissing or discrediting the natural sciences or evolutionary theory, for they are integral to his empirical order of inquiry. He questions evolutionism in the same spirit that we today question social Darwinism. When James writes "a current toward healthy-mindedness far more important and interesting than that which sets in from natural science is the mind-cure movement," it would be a mistake to assume that he rejects the empirical claims of natural science. On the contrary, as Joan Richardson observes, "His signal contribution was to articulate the identity of aesthetic with religious experience within the Darwinian framework, in his examples and explanations naturalizing and legitimizing this experience as an 'organ' with the functions of any other organ."[77] James does not reject natural sciences and the Darwinian framework; what concerns him are how they are used, and what values are created. The problem with evolutionism for James is that it does not offer anything above or beyond medical materialism. Evolutionism encourages a systematization of happiness, which is tantamount to a systematized blindness to psychic diversity. It is a kind of optimization. But is the mind an organ only or primarily designed for achieving happy good health?

The mind-cure movement offers another way of moving with the natural sciences. James locates the "doctrinal sources of Mind-cure [in] the four Gospels; another is Emersonianism or New England transcendentalism; another is Berkeleyan idealism; another is spiritism, with its messages of 'law' and 'progress' and 'development'; another the optimistic popular science evolutionism of which I have recently spoken; and, finally, Hinduism has contributed a strain." He finds in the movement "traces of Christian mysticism, of transcendental idealism, of vedantism, and of the modern psychology of the subliminal self."[78] What particularly interests James about the mind-cure movement is its transformation of sciences. First, the movement implies an energetic model of the psyche in its claim that "the cause of sickness and weakness and depression is human sense of separateness from Divine Energy."[79] For James, thinking in terms of energy also presents an improvement over the rationalist stance characteristic of dialectics. He notes that "mind-cure has developed a living system of mental hygiene which may well claim to have thrown all previous literature of the *Diätetik der Seele* into the shade."[80]

Second, what attracts James to this movement lies in how "it carries on an aggressive warfare against the scientific philosophy, and succeeds by using science's own peculiar methods and weapons."[81] In other words, James sees in the mind-cure movement a resistance to rationalism (scientific philosophy and dialectics) through its adoption of experimental methods. He confirms as much in his later summary: "The mind-cure gospel thus once more appears to us as having dignity and importance. We have seen it to be a genuine religion, and no mere silly appeal to imagination to cure disease; we have seen its method of experimental verification to be not unlike the method of all science; and now here we find mind-cure as the champion of a perfectly definite conception of the metaphysical structure of the world."[82] Ultimately, then, the mind-cure movement suggests to James an empirically and pragmatically better way of working with natural science, geared toward energetics and the experimental method, both of which imply a principle of satisfaction.

The mind-cure movement might be said to discover the plane of consistency for the natural sciences by digging below the ground of scientific rationalism (efficient reason) to uncover the truer principle of natural science, that is, satisfaction. What is more, the mind-cure movement becomes a genuine religion in the sense of allowing for an experience of the absolute. It is here, however, that the mind-cure movement reaches its limit. It delineates the domain of the absolute in terms of health and cure. It falls back on health, settles for cure. In effect, James tells us, this is as far as we seem to be able to go today with health. The mind curers push toward the absolute yet settle for relativizing, that is, reterritorializing our health, our bodies, our minds. They place territorial limits on diversity in the name of health and cure. In this sense, the mind-cure movement ultimately falls back on the physical, materialistic world.

The mind-cure movement in James may be said to play a role similar to that of the crystal in Simondon. For Simondon, the model of crystalliza-tion allows him to establish a transcendental field for individuation with-out positing a substantialist divide between different modes of existence, such as physical beings (crystal) and living beings (plant). Simondon sees an ontological difference between physical beings and living beings. The difference between a physical being like a crystal and a living being like a plant is that the plant carries more of its associated milieu with it. A crystal stops growing when you remove it from its aqueous solution. A plant may stop growing if you do not water it, but it carries a good deal of water with it, which allows for greater regulation of the relation between its inner and external milieus. It even puts water into circulation within its ecology. It draws on the preindividual reserves it carries with it to prolong its phas-ing. Simondon reminds us that the path of evolution from physical being to living being is not teleological or dialectical. In effect, the plant emerges when the crystal becomes inchoate, unable to prolong its structure. Its form is turned inside out and reorganized around other material flows to prolong the transindividual relation.

In a like manner, although James sees in the mind-cure movement a pathway toward thinking in terms of individuation and excavating the plane of consistency of natural science, he also sees how the mind-cure movement remains content to act on the relation between psychic center of energy and margin. It achieves no more than a simple classical equilibrium. If James wishes to radicalize what he finds in the mind-cure movement, it is because he takes seriously the claims of what is left outside the domain of healthy-mindedness, those psychic variations that today are the domain of neurodiversity. The mind-cure movement loses sight of the process of individuation and thus the diversity it initially brings to the fore. It tends to rule out pathological and exceptional states, where preindividual being and transmarginal becoming are activated—equilibrium away from equilibrium. This is why James does not merely dismiss or drop the mind-cure movement. To move beyond it, he must go deeper into it. He must find the higher and vaster principle within it, in the same way that a living being finds the vaster and deeper principle of individuation within the crystal—transindividuality in Simondon, the transmarginal region in James.

It is of the greatest significance that James associates diversity with evil, and the transmarginal with natural aberration. He does so first when addressing the mind-cure movement. He notes how "the mind-curers, so far as I am acquainted with them, profess to give no speculative explanation. Evil is empirically there for them as it is for everybody, but the practical point of view dominates. . . . [Evil] is something merely to be outgrown and left behind, transcended and forgotten."[83] Needless to say, James does not feel evil should be forgotten; nor can it be outgrown or transcended.[84] On the positive side, because the mind curers do not bother with a speculative explanation for evil, they bypass the rationalist mode of explanation in which evil may be considered necessary for the advance of the good. Evil for rationalism is something out there for God to overcome, gradually, rationally, dialectically. In contrast, if James is to stick to the facts of aberration and ill-adaptation—the machine that works by breaking down—he must allow for genuine exteriority and leave room for "inner" diversity, immanent variation. This is why he turns to those people for whom evil is not something out there, but something in here, in them, in us. Still, the problem of rationalizing evil will persist if it is merely internalized. At the risk of reducing the complexity of his argumentation, let me note that this is ultimately the gift of the saint for James: the saint does not rationalize or internalize evil; the saint acknowledges something wrong with the world, and even something wrong with herself, which cannot be overcome or forgotten. If the saint arrives at a new kind of joy beyond physical happiness, it is because she feels how the struggle with evil is what opens the world to a force of becoming. This evil means we do not live in the best of all possible worlds, and yet it is possible to believe in this world.

Nevertheless, for James, pure saintliness is not the answer. He does not seek salvation from a fallen condition in the manner of Heidegger, by dwelling in the rupture that might reveal the depths of Being. For James, the significance of the saint lies in how she pushes religious experience to its absolute limit by shattering doctrines, theism, the theological reason operative in religious institutions. At the same time, the saint is, in effect, a force of the past, a pressure on the present in which mind cure is the limit on which we have settled. The saintly today becomes manifest (and is activated) through what are presently ruled out as exceptional and pathological states. Yesterday's saintliness becomes madness at the turn of the twentieth century and neurodiversity at the turn of the twenty-first.[85] At the same time, although there are important sites of intersection with the Freudian method, James does not approach such psychological diversity in terms of an original constitutive lack in the manner of some schools of psychoanalysis. Instead of original lack conceptualized in terms of an enclosed or walled-up psyche, James finds material flows organized around a contingent impurity—energetic systems. For such reasons, James opts neither for the mind cure nor for the saint. He tracks their tendencies and limits to consider what socially and psychically marginal experiences might do in the contemporary situation.

In this way, his thinking is ecological. Instead of focusing on external determination or conditions of possibility, his thinking gravitates toward the transindividual or transmarginal force through which various components of a system come into relation through a process of individuation, the dephasing of a metastable state in relation to a contingent impurity. A system, then, entails a neutral point neither inside nor outside the system, what James elsewhere calls a "little absolute." This is why James gravitates toward religious experience; it opens the question of the absolute he is so concerned with. While he reminds us that religious experience is a kind of experience (it is not different in nature from experience in general), it highlights a relation to the absolute, which opens a way to put the absolute back into relation. Famously, James rejects grand absolutes or the Absolute. If he insists on the "inward" direction of religious experience, it is to deal with the little absolutes that arise through "natural" diversity— selection and transformation based on immanent variation. This is where ecological thinking happens.

The Admissibility of Belief

Revisiting James's *Varieties of Religious Experience*, Charles Taylor concludes that the present era is Jamesian. Taylor's approach depends on situating James's work historically, or more precisely, within the history of ideas. He thus highlights James's contribution to one of the key debates of modernity—over the admissibility of belief. James clearly places himself on the side of those who admit belief into the domain of modern scientific inquiry, against those who see only one road to truth, one that precludes belief. Taylor aptly characterizes James's stance thus: "James holds, on the contrary, that there are some domains in which truths will be hidden from us unless we go at least halfway toward them. Do you like me or not?" Indeed, Taylor declares, James might be seen as arguing for a "right to believe."[86]

As a philosopher dedicated to the question of modernity, Taylor understands groundlessness to be the quintessentially modern experience. As such, Taylor expresses keen sympathy for James's approach, singing his praises in those terms: "James is our great philosopher of the cusp. He tells us more than anyone else about what it's like to stand in that open space and feel the winds pulling you now here, now there." Yet, as the title of his intervention—*Varieties of Religion Today*—attests, his concerns lie more with religion than with experience. Because, like Durkheim, Taylor associates religious institutions with collective life, he worries about how James tends to strip away received forms, not only received psychological forms but also the traditional forms of religious mediation. He notes, "First, precisely because he [James] abandons so much of the traditional ground of religion, because he has no use for collective connections through sacraments or ways of life, because the intellectual articulations are made secondary, the key point—what to make of the gut instinct that there is something more?—stands out very clearly." Second, however, Taylor worries that when James establishes his transcendental field, he leaves us with only an experience of groundlessness, without any received ideas (forms) to guide us. Thus, Taylor adds, "as you stand on the cusp, all you have to go on is a (very likely poorly articulated) gut feeling."[87]

Because Taylor's history of ideas proceeds dialectically, he takes care to situate James in relation to an opposing force, which he draws from Durkheim. Thus, Taylor puts forward three "ideal types" based on Durkheim: paleo-, neo-, and post-Durkheimian moments.[88] Sometimes Taylor calls these ideal types "ages" or "eras," and sometimes he calls them "dispositions." But the aim of his history of ideas is to establish a contradiction: where our era or disposition might be deemed Jamesian, James's era was thoroughly Durkheimian. Where James confronted and philosophically contested the ground under Durkheimian conditions, today those Durkheimian conditions have largely disappeared. Elsewhere they may be renewed, in a neo-Durkheimian manner. Yet, in North America at least,

Taylor submits, our contemporary disposition is at once Jamesian (right to believe) and post-Durkheimian (loss of traditional religious forms).

This new disposition presents problems James could not have foreseen, in Taylor's opinion. For Taylor, then, the fundamental question no longer concerns James, strictly speaking. At stake is a contemporary disposition that, because at once Jamesian and post-Durkheimian, implies a contradiction: the "right to believe" now comes to the fore without any traditional forms of religious or political mediation in place. Taylor describes this disposition thus: "This expressive individualism, which has been growing since the war, is obviously stronger in some milieus than others, stronger among youth than among older people, stronger among those who were formed in the 1960s and 1970s; but overall it seems steadily to advance." It remains indifferent to external demands and authority, which Taylor associates with collective life, especially that offered by religious institutions like the church (but also political frameworks like the public sphere). He explains, "In the post-Durkheimian age, many people are un-comprehending in face of the demand to conform. . . . For many people today, to set aside their own path in order to conform to some external authority just doesn't seem comprehensible as a form of spiritual life."[89]

If I linger on Taylor's account, it is because the debate over the admissibility of belief has the potential to bring us onto a more complex terrain of power, where varieties of experience matter. But we will have to look at this debate from another perspective.

Radical Historicism

Taylor reads the debate over the admissibility of belief in terms of a rather static contradiction between the Jamesian and the Durkheimian. James's method, however, always invites us to think more dynamically about contradiction, to think of it less in terms of a rational or dialectical movement (in relation to a Grand Absolute or transcendent point of view) and more in terms of "energetic" or transversal movement, in relation to a little absolute (neutral point). In this respect, James's approach feels compatible with Foucault's. Indeed, the debate over belief may be read genealogically, in a Foucauldian manner.

The unresolved and perhaps unresolvable question remains: Is belief inadmissible or admissible within modern knowledge production? Taylor strives to resolve the question dialectically: yes, belief is admissible, but only if mediated through the external authorities of our received institutions of religion and government. Indeed, Taylor feels that, when James formulated his concept of pure experience, religious institutions were still firmly enough in place to ensure overall social stability. Today, however, in Taylor's opinion, the right to believe presents a destabilizing force that takes the form of an individualist stance. He writes, "The new framework has a strongly individualist component, but this will not necessarily mean that the content will be individuating. Many people will find themselves joining extremely powerful religious communities."[90] In other words, Taylor portrays the historical trajectory of James's right to believe in terms of an individualizing form without content, which inadvertently spurs a desire for exceedingly conformist communities.

Taylor finds in received religious institutions some sort of reasonable balance, or rational relation, between form and content, whose authority should be accepted as precedent, as the ground, for contemporary dispositions. As in Durkheim, by reference to the ground (the Church-State formation Taylor deems characteristic of Western civilization), Taylor transforms the relation between form and content (roots and fruits) into one of rational representation. True to the Hegelian stance wherein the real is the rational (instead of the relational), Taylor wishes to establish the primacy of reason (rationalism), to the point where empiricism (diversity of sciences) and pragmatism (belief) may no longer lay claim to reality. Rationalism, as a civilizing mission, makes reason into morality and then claims that this moral reason is at once the cause and the effect of the proper (Western) balance of religion and government that will someday ground modern society.

The debate over the admissibility of belief, then, is genealogically entwined with questions about sovereignty, not to mention Western civilization. James's call for the admissibility of belief is not about rights or individualism, as Taylor would have us think. James's call is akin to Foucault's call to "cut off the head of the king" in our analyses of power.[91] Foucault's point is that we should not begin our analyses with so-called natural sovereignty, either of the monarch or the modern individual. In effect, in James's account of religious experience, he has cut off the head of the king—or the head of the Church—natural sovereignty. This move allows James, on the one hand, to take seriously the mind-cure movement and to evaluate other religious movements of his day beyond a stark contrast between Protestantism and Catholicism. On the other hand, James's movement of thought is sustained through his critique of pure saintliness, prolonged through careful consideration of the groundless ground afforded by the natural sciences. For James, then, reason and rationalism are not the constant point of reference (or the ground) for an analysis of experience. By the same token, so-called natural sovereignty does not supply the sole point of reference (or the prepositive ground for) analyses of power.

As such, unlike Durkheim and Taylor, James and Foucault do not endorse what might be called a massive modernity thesis—in the form of civilization or Rationalization. They engage with diverse fields of rationality, precisely because looking at power in terms of a massive Rationalization—such as civilization, modernization, or globalization—will ultimately naturalize the claims of reason and rationalism over and above those of empirical sciences and pragmatic beliefs. This is not to say that James (or Foucault) wishes to dispense with reason or rationalism. James presents a method for thinking both the "individuating" stance of empiricism (natural sciences) and the pragmatic stance on the admissibility of belief (religious experience). Thinking across empiricism and pragmatism allows James to resituate the claims of rationalism, empirically and pragmatically, which paves the way for his third order of inquiry—pluralism. It is pluralism that permits James to think in terms of diverse fields of rationality rather than the massive modernity thesis of Rationalization. Here, radical empiricism may join forces with radical historicism.

James thus has a good deal to offer contemporary analyses of experience and of power. Oddly enough, many contemporary media studies that lay claim to a Jamesian perspective tend to reach an impasse when fields of rationality are in question. Because they address computational, digital, and hence mathematical fields of rationality, their critique tends to focus on a principle of efficient reason. Thus, questions of power are primarily posed in terms of a critique of technological optimization, which implies a kind of massive modernity thesis (modernization or globalization) as well as its Eurocentric stance. Such a stance proves that a Heideggerian era is in effect, instead of Jamesian. Such a stance makes it difficult and maybe impossible to consider, as James does, how forms of individualization or personalization allow us to understand the principle of satisfaction at work in diverse fields of rationality, in diverse politics as well as the politics of diversity.

In the spirit of providing a kind of biophysiology or ecology of power for media studies, I would like to conclude by considering briefly how

James's method invites us to situate questions of power within fields of rationality—in contrast to the focus on dialectical reason in Taylor or the critique of efficient reason in Heidegger.

Coda: Superordination

Lapoujade's account of James has inspired me to work through the ways in which James approaches the individuation happening within the individualized psyche by using energetic terms analogous to those in Simondon: (1) margin, or external milieu; (2) center of energy, or form; (3) energy at center, or preindividual being turned toward the internal milieu; and (4) transmarginal region, or associated milieu with transindividual being. Recall that James claims that we can only understand an individual (a psyche, a plant, an experience) if we look at it in its environment and out of it. Such a procedure highlights a disjunctive relation between roots and fruits—the plant is pulled out with dirt clinging to its roots. The relation between roots and fruits is not one of resemblance or representation, and likewise with the relation between margin (temperament) and the center of energy (character) of the psyche. A dirty region comes between, appears everywhere, a region of heterogeneous scales. The heterogenous stuff of dirt hangs together at its edges. Likewise, the overall coordination of the living system—plant or psyche—might be said to coordinate by hanging together at the edges, which allows for an overall coordination.

As such, while it is possible to speak of external or environmental determinants—what Durkheim calls "social facts" and Taylor calls "external authorities"—these determinants present blockages that make possible flows through the system in the making. So-called environmental determinants thus become functions inside the system, internal variation. Yet there is no relation of resemblance or representation between the so-called external facts and the overall direction of the system. Internal variation is, in fact, *immanent* variation. As such, the question of power, which is still posed almost exclusively in terms of external determinants (dominance and dominants), has to be posed differently, in light of immanent variation. Here it is a matter not just of domination (natural sovereignty), but also of something like subordination.

As heterogeneous flows and functions are coordinated, in a movement of concatenation, for instance, there is also subordination. As James remarks, "Thus the lowest grade of universe would be a world of mere withness, of which the parts were only strung together by the conjunction 'and.' Such a universe is even now the collection of our several inner lives. . . . But add our sensations and bodily actions, and the union mounts to a much higher grade."[92] The term "subordination" may be misleading, however, if it is taken to mean only or primarily the domination of one flow or function over another. The process might better be called "superordination" or "superpositioning."[93] Here, ordination or position implies at once "overness" and "withness." The organism is more like a "superject" of its environment than a subject. As Brian Massumi explains, "The subject is the subjective form, or dynamic unity, of the extra-effecting event."[94] Because this sort of superordination, or superjection, is a matter of satisfaction not optimization, degrees (margins, latitudes, magnitudes) are at stake.

This is where the question of power might be posed anew. External determinants, those ever-enticing social facts and algorithms, act with and through satisfying the need for the superordination of functions, arriving only within an ecology and acting through a subject that is a superject. Taylor captures something of this possibility when he hesitates to order historical "dispositions" teleologically or even dialectically. Dispositions, like the Foucauldian *dispositif*, arise through superpositioning of functions that somehow add up to an overall coordination, a kind of open system. When it comes to religious experience, for instance, Foucault offers a genealogical series: pastoral power, biopower, neoliberal power. Or is it pastoral power (confessional), sexuality, criminalization? It might also be pastoral power, racial territory, security. The series diverges; it bifurcates and generates new superpositionings, new superjects, other satisfactions on fields of rationality. Each field has its facts to take into account and its criteria for success and failure.

James's account of religious experience, with its ontogenetic approach, does not provide the same degree of logical inquiry into phylogenetic or genealogical variation as Foucault's does. Nevertheless, its variety of instances and attention to variation should give pause to contemporary media studies, science and technology studies, and cultural studies. These fields of inquiry should not rest content to bypass or ignore questions about individualization and the fields of rationality emerging through claims to satisfaction. They should not rest content with what both James and Foucault rejected: the massive modernity thesis in its various guises— civilization and Rationalization, modernization and globalization. Nor should they be content with the critique of efficient reason, using it to ignore the critique of pure saintliness. Such fields might benefit from applying the method of natural diversity (empiricism) and the admissibility of belief (pragmatism) to produce a fuller, more diverse politics of diversity (pluralism). This is the path of ecological thinking, now stretched across radical empiricism (ontogenesis) and radical historicism (phylogenesis), with keen attention to the pragmatic value of subjectivities (selves in the making) and existential territories (fields of rationality).

Notes

PREFACE ✓

1. Isabelle Stengers, *Thinking with Whitehead: A Free and Wild Creation of Concepts*, trans. Michael Chase (Cambridge, MA: Harvard University Press, 2011).

2. David Lapoujade, *Fictions du pragmatisme: William et Henry James* (Paris: Les Éditions du minuit, 2008); Stéphane Madelrieux, *William James: L'attitude empiriste* (Paris: Presses Universitaires de France, 2008).

3. Stéphane Madelrieux, ed., *Bergson et James: Cent an après* (Paris: Presses Universitaires de France, 2011).

4. David Lapoujade, *Powers of Time / Potências do tempo*, trans. Andrew Goffey (Sao Paulo: N-1 Publications, 2013).

5. William James, *The Varieties of Religious Experience*, in *The Works of William James*, electronic ed. (Charlottesville, VA: InteLex, 2008), 26.

6. *Varieties*, 295.

7. See John E. Smith's introduction to *The Varieties of Religious Experience* (Harvard University Press, 1985), xvii.

8. Lapoujade, *Fictions du pragmatisme*, 7.

9. Lapoujade, *Fictions du pragmatisme*, 15.

INTRODUCTION

1. William James, *Pragmatism*, in *The Works of William James*, electronic ed. (Charlottesville, VA: InteLex, 2008), 104. Emphasis in the original.

2. Max Horkeimer, *The Eclipse of Reason* (New York: Continuum, 1992), 52. See also the first chapter of Ludwig Marcuse's work *La philosophie américaine* (Paris: Gallimard, 1967), 8–45, where the author notably quotes Bertrand Russell's phrase, "I find love of truth is obscured in America by commercialism, of which pragmatism is the philosophical expression," from "As a European Radical Sees It," *Freeman* 4 (March 8, 1922): 610.

3. In a letter to H. G. Wells, September 11, 1906, James denounces "the moral flabbiness born of the exclusive worship of the bitch-Goddess SUCCESS. That— with the squalid cash interpretation put on the word success—is our national

disease." *The Correspondence of William James*, electronic ed., 19 vols. (Charlottesville, VA: InteLex, 2008), 11:267.

4. James, *A Pluralistic Universe*, in *Works of William James*, 117. Emphasis in the original.

5. James was born in 1842. He initially directed his studies toward physiology and medicine, but under the impetus of Wilhelm Maximillian Wundt and Hermann von Helmholtz, whom he admired, he turned toward psychophysiology. From 1877, after becoming a teacher, he published his first important essays. Most of the articles from this period, with revisions, formed the basis, after some twelve years of work, for the publication of *Principles of Psychology* (1890). Soon to follow were *The Will to Believe* (1897), *The Varieties of Religious Experience* (1902), *Pragmatism* (1907), and *The Idea of Truth and Philosophy of Experience* (1907). He died in 1910, leaving an unfinished work, *Introduction to Philosophy*, and a series of articles collected under the title *Essays in Radical Empiricism*.

6. In "How to Make Our Ideas Clear," Peirce writes, "The rule for attaining the third grade of clearness of apprehension is as follows: Consider what effects, that might conceivably have practical bearings, we conceive the object of our conception to have. Then, our conception of these effects is the whole of our conception of the object." *The Writings of Charles S. Peirce—A Chronological Edition*, electronic ed. (Charlottesville, VA: InteLex, 2003), 3:266.

7. *Pragmatism*, 37. See, too, Emmanuel Leroux, *Le pragmatisme américain et anglais: Étude historique et critique* (Paris: Alcan, 1922), 163n2. In 1904 pragmatism only designated a method (undoubtedly because of the influence of Peirce), and the term "humanism" was reserved for the theory of truth (because of the influence of Schiller), as is evident in James's *The Meaning of Truth*, in *The Works of William James*. If James happens to speak of "pragmatist philosophers," it is simply for tactical reasons, to make pragmatism into a war machine against rival philosophical currents. In a letter to Wilhelm Jerusalem on September 15, 1907, he writes, "Pragmatism is an unlucky word in some respects, and the two meanings I give for it are somewhat heterogeneous. But it was already in vogue in France and Italy as well as in England and America, and it was *tactically* advantageous to use it" (*Correspondence*, 11:448).

8. *The Will to Believe and Other Essays in Popular Philosophy*, in *Works of William James*, 78.

9. A note on transcendentalism and Anglo-Saxon Hegelianism: under the influence of Thomas Carlyle, the transcendentalism of Samuel Taylor Coleridge and Ralph Waldo Emerson gravitated toward the thinking of a Whole-Nature inspired by German Romanticism, as was the case with William James's father, whose philosophy drew a great deal of inspiration from Emanuel Swedenborg. All things tend to merge, becoming absorbed in the great unity God-Nature. The subsequent confusion of the transcendentalist themes of Fusion and the Over-Soul (Emerson) with Hegelian philosophy made for a favorable reception of Hegel. J. H. Stirling's *The Secret of Hegel* (1865), the most detailed study, would have considerable influence on the next generation. A new school developed around the *Journal*

of Speculative Thought, founded by William T. Harris, with T. H. Green and the Caird brothers, Edward and John, as major contributors. The American use of Hegel was primarily concerned with the notion of totality—under the influence of transcendentalism—while largely ignoring dialectical progress. Not until Royce (a friend and colleague of James) published *The World and the Individual* (1899–1901), and the Englishman Francis H. Bradley published *Appearance and Reality* (1893), did a more rigorous development of Hegelianism appear, based on a logic of relations, entirely different from Hegel. These are the thinkers that James takes on when he issues his challenge to absolutism. On these questions, see Hubert W. Schneider, *A History of American Philosophy* (New York: Columbia University Press, 1946), 477; Gérard Deledalle, *La philosophie américaine* (Lausanne: De Boeck University, 1983); and Leroux, *Le pragmatisme américain*, beginning at p. 19.

10. Ralph Waldo Emerson, "History," in *The Collected Works of Ralph Waldo Emerson*, vol. 2, *Essays, First Series*, electronic ed. (Charlottesville, VA: InteLex, 2008), 44.

11. On these questions, see Schneider, *History of American Philosophy*, especially chapters 3 and 5; and Deledalle, *La philosophie américaine*, 36: "Emerson insists on this last point: having confidence in yourself, is to have confidence in humanity, in all humanity." On Henry James Sr., see Deledalle, *La philosophie américaine*, 43–45.

12. James went through a similar crisis, as he confides in a letter to Oliver Wendell Holmes, September 17, 1867: "My external history . . . resembles that of a sea anemone." Subsequently he speaks of the "deadness of spirit thereby produced" (*Correspondence*, 4:220).

13. *Pragmatism*, 44: "But you see already how democratic she [pragmatism] is."

1. RADICAL EMPIRICISM

1. David Hume, *An Enquiry Concerning Human Understanding* (Toronto: Broadview, 2011), 72.

2. James, *Principles of Psychology*, in *The Works of William James*, 263. Emphasis mine.

3. *Principles of Psychology*, 261.

4. Edmund Husserl, *Cartesian Meditations*, trans. Dorion Cairns (The Hague: Martinus Nijhoff, 1960), 38–39.

5. James, *Essays in Radical Empiricism*, in *The Works of William James*, 81.

6. *Essays in Radical Empiricism*, 4.

7. *Essays in Radical Empiricism*, 114: "This will be a monism, if you will, but an exceedingly basic monism absolutely opposed to the so-called bilateral monism of scientific or Spinozist positivism." Translator's note: One of the essays collected in *Essays in Radical Empiricism* appears in French. "La Notion de Conscience" was delivered at the 5th International Congress of Psychology in Rome, April 30, 1905. I here translate James's French original cited by the author into English.

8. This is the meaning of a profound remark by Bergson to James, February 15, 1905: "The existence of some reality outside all actual consciousness is certainly not the existence *in itself* touted by the old substantialism; and yet it is not actually

presented to a consciousness, it is something intermediate between the two, always on the verge of coming into consciousness or coming back into consciousness, something intimately mingled with conscious life, *interwoven with it*, and not *underlying it*, as substantialism would have it." From "Mélanges," trans. Melissa McMahon, in *Henri Bergson: Key Writings*, ed. Keith Ansell Pearson and John Mullarkey (New York: Continuum, 2002), 359.

9. *Essays in Radical Empiricism*, 4. Emphasis mine.

10. *Essays in Radical Empiricism*, 29: "Knowledge of sensible realities thus comes to life inside the tissue of experience." See too *The Meaning of Truth*, in *The Works of William James*, 80: "But it and the object are both of them bits of the general sheet and tissue of reality at large." We should recall too that "material" in English means not only material but cloth or fabric as well, literally (as in dress materials) and figuratively (he is champion material). The same goes for "stuff." In this sense, Bergson is right to use the verb "interwoven."

11. *Essays in Radical Empiricism*, 113. Original essay in French. See note 7 above. In *The Analysis of Mind* (1921), Bertrand Russell would propose a "neutral monism" drawing inspiration from James—yet equally influenced by Whitehead. See, too, Bertrand Russell, *My Philosophical Development* (London: Allen and Unwin, 1959), as well as Ali Benmakhlouf's study, *Bertrand Russell, L'atomisme logique*, Philosophie 70 (Paris: Presses Universitaires de France, 1996), 71–75.

12. James's article appeared in 1904, *Matter and Memory* in 1896. In a letter to Bergson dated December 14, 1902, James reports that he read Bergson's work at the time of its publication, and reading it again recently, found its points essential: "The *Hauptpunkt* acquired for me is your conclusive demolition of the dualism of object and subject in perception. I believe that the 'transcendency' of the object will not recover from your treatment, and as I myself have been working for many years past on the same line, only with other general conceptions than yours, I find myself most agreeably corroborated." (*Correspondence*, 10:167).

13. Bergson writes, "It is true that an image may *be* without *being perceived*, it may be presented without being represented." *Matter and Memory*, trans. N. M. Paul and W. S. Palmer (New York: Zone, 1988), 35. Emphasis in original.

14. Bergson, *Matter and Memory*, 38–39.

15. *Manuscript Essays and Notes*, in *The Works of William James*, 18 (entry 4459).

16. Émile Durkheim, *Pragmatism and Sociology*, trans. J. C. Whitehouse (Cambridge: Cambridge University Press, 1983), 35: "What characterizes radical empiricism is its emphasis upon the absolute uniformity of existence. It refuses to admit the idea that there are two worlds, that of experience and that of reality."

17. This expression is borrowed from Deleuze, who proposes, "Transcendental empiricism is the only way to avoid tracing the transcendental from the outlines of the empirical." *Difference and Repetition*, trans. Paul Patton (New York: Columbia University Press, 1994), 144. In an entirely different context, Deleuze puts forward a transcendental field without self or intentionality, entirely shot through with multiplicities. See *The Logic of Sense*, trans. Mark Lester (London: Athlone Press, 1990), 102–5. Deleuze and Guattari call for a radical empiricism in *What Is*

Philosophy? trans. Hugh Tomlinson and Graham Burchell (New York: Columbia University Press, 1994), 47: "When immanence is no longer immanent to something other than itself it is possible to speak of a plane of immanence. Such a plane is, perhaps, a radical empiricism."

18. F. W. J. Schelling had already undertaken a similar enterprise with his "philosophical empiricism." The philosophy of nature has for its ambition to establish the pure fact of the world. It aims for a universal subject-objectivity, but one that is not to be established either by the subject or in the object. Schelling introduces *between* subject and object a milieu, a "sort of point of indifference" situated on the magnetic line linking the two poles. Each point on the line expresses its median or indifferent point at the same time as its bipolarity. "In the entire universe there is nothing absolutely subjective or objective; in accordance to that with which it is compared, the same thing may be subjective or objective." Here we find mental-physical material as a reality intermediary between subject and object, the "universal polarities of nature." Yet Schelling then introduces a hylomorphic schema, subjecting the process of this line to the Pythagorean pair of limited/ unlimited, which will constitute two of the terms of divine triplicity. See "Exposé de l'empirisme philosophique," *Philosophie*, no. 40 (1993): 4–23.

19. *Principles of Psychology*, 219–20. Emphasis in original.

20. Sartre first notes that Husserl doubles the psychological self within the transcendental in the form of an I, a structure of absolute consciousness. He criticizes this gesture, which he considers useless. See Jean-Paul Sartre, *La transcendence de l'ego* (Paris: Vrin, 1966). On the Kantian double, see Mikel Dufrenne, *La notion d'a priori* (Paris: Presses Universitaires de France, 1959), 20–21. It should be noted that James did not comment on Husserl (with whom he was not familiar); my remarks here, and the previous ones, are based entirely on James's critique of psychology.

21. Kant writes, "Metaphysics as well as pure philosophy grounds its knowledge, above all, in *forms of thought*. . . . The possibility of all synthetic knowledge rests on these forms." "On a Newly Arisen Superior Tone in Philosophy," trans. Peter Fenves, in *Raising the Tone of Philosophy* (Baltimore: Johns Hopkins University Press, 1993), 70. Emphasis in original.

22. This passage appears in a letter from Bergson to James, dated February 15, 1905, reprinted in Henri Bergson, *Sur le pragmatisme de William James*, ed. Stéphane Madelrieux (Paris: Presses Universitaires de France, 2011), 63. Emphasis in the original.

23. *Essays in Radical Empiricism*, 46.

24. *Essays in Radical Empiricism*, 73. Emphasis in original.

25. *Essays in Radical Empiricism*, 36.

26. *Principles of Psychology*, 233–34.

27. *Principles of Psychology*, 322.

28. *Principles of Psychology*, 279: "But it is clear that between what a man calls *me* and what he simply calls *mine* the line is difficult to draw. . . . *In its widest possible sense*, however, *a man's Self is the sum total of all that he* can *call his*." Emphasis in original.

29. *Essays in Radical Empiricism*, 8–9.

30. We should also take note of the ambiguity of Saussure's dyad: the signifier sometimes refers to a signified (as mental content), sometimes to an objective referent. See Émile Benveniste, *Problèmes de linguistique générale*, tome I (Paris: Gallimard, 1966), 1:49–55.

31. Peirce, *Collected Papers*, 5.284. In Peirce's classification, the interpretant may equally well be an emotion (affective interpretant), a physical or mental effort (dynamic interpretant), or a habit (logical interpretant), all of which are signs (5.475–76). In keeping with the accepted format for citing Peirce, I use the numbering system from his *Collected Papers*, ed. Charles Hartshorne and Paul Weiss (Cambridge, MA: Harvard University Press, 1994). I am also drawing here on the two works, whose remarkable analyses I have considerably simplified: Claudine Tiercelin, *La pensée-signe: Etudes sur C. S. Peirce* (Nîmes: J. Chambon, 1993); and Christiane Chauviré, *Peirce et la signification: introduction à la logique du vague* (Paris: Presses Universitaires de France, 1995).

32. Durkheim, *Pragmatism and Sociology*, 42. If Durkheim takes issue with pragmatism, James has his own reservations about Durkheim's theses.

33. *Principles of Psychology*, 913 and 924. Emphasis in original.

34. *Principles of Psychology*, 946 and 928. Emphasis in original.

35. Consider, too, Peirce's definition in "How to Make Our Ideas Clear": "Thus we may define the real as that whose characters are independent of what anybody may think them to be."

36. See, too, *The Meaning of Truth*, 45: "If our own particular thought were annihilated the reality would still be there in some shape, tho possibly it might be a shape that would lack something that our thought supplies."

37. *The Meaning of Truth*, 45. Emphasis mine.

38. *The Meaning of Truth*, 43.

39. *Essays in Radical Empiricism*, 19. Similar formulations already make an appearance in *Principles of Psychology*, for instance: "The sense of my bodily existence, however obscurely recognized as such, *may* then be the absolute original of my conscious selfhood, the fundamental perception that *I am*. All appropriations *may* be made *to* it, *by* a Thought not at the moment immediately cognized by itself" (323). Emphasis in original.

40. Bergson, *Matter and Memory*, 14–15.

41. *Essays in Radical Empiricism*, 85.

42. *Principles of Psychology*, 247: "This field of view of consciousness varies very much in extent, depending largely on the degree of mental freshness or fatigue. When very fresh, our minds carry an immense horizon with them. . . . And in states of extreme brain-fog the horizon is narrowed almost to the passing word."

43. Peirce undertakes an analogous enterprise in his semiology, as Tiercelin stresses in *La pensée-signe*: "It thus becomes clear that the central concept in Peircean semiology is not in fact that of representation, . . . nor even that of the sign, but rather 'sign in act.'" The classification of signs "only makes sense in the

light of semiosis, and the functions that the sign may perform in it" (194–96). Similarly, Deledalle writes in his afterword to a collection of Peirce's texts, *Écrits sur le signe* (Paris: Éditions du Seuil, 1978), "The signification of the sign is tied to the action of the sign, not to the sign as such" (222).

44. *Essays in Radical Empiricism*, 61 and 64. Emphasis in the original.

45. *Essays in Radical Empiricism*, 4: "Let me then immediately explain that I mean only to deny that the word stands for an entity, but to insist most emphatically that it does stand for a function."

2. TRUTH AND KNOWLEDGE

1. *The Will to Believe*, 24.

2. *Pragmatism*, 102.

3. *A Pluralistic Universe*, 122–23n1. Emphasis in original.

4. *Pragmatism*, 42. Emphasis in original.

5. Russell works through various stages of his exchanges with James while intermittently using these two articles, A and B, to recapitulate all his objections against pragmatism in "The Definition of 'Truth,'" chapter 15 of *My Philosophical Development*, 180–81.

6. *Pragmatism*, 97. Emphasis in original.

7. *The Meaning of Truth*, 54.

8. *Pragmatism*, 37: "Our thoughts become true in proportion as they successfully exert their go-between function."

9. *Pragmatism*, 104. Emphasis in original.

10. *Pragmatism*, 35: "New truth is always a go-between, a smoother-over of transitions."

11. *The Meaning of Truth*, 222–23.

12. *Pragmatism*, 97. Emphasis in original.

13. *Some Problems of Philosophy*, in *The Works of William James*, 37: "Now however beautiful or otherwise worthy of stationary contemplation the substantive part of a concept may be, the more important part of its significance may naturally be held to be the consequences to which it leads. These may lie either in the way of *making us think*, or in the way of making us act." Emphasis mine.

14. *The Meaning of Truth*, 111, 113.

15. *The Will to Believe*, 67: "The permanent presence of the sense of futurity in the mind has been strangely ignored by most writers, but the fact is that our consciousness at a given moment is never free from the ingredient of expectancy."

16. *Pragmatism*, 100. Emphasis in original.

17. *Varieties*, 189: "As our mental fields succeed one another, each has its centre of interest, around which the objects of which we are less and less attentively conscious fade to a margin so faint that its limits are unassignable."

18. *The Meaning of Truth*, 67–68.

19. *The Meaning of Truth*, 50

20. *The Meaning of Truth*, 110.

21. *A Pluralistic Universe*, 145: "Pragmatically interpreted, pluralism or the doctrine that it is many means only that the sundry parts of reality *may be externally related.*" Emphasis in original.

22. *The Meaning of Truth*, 136: "Abstraction . . . becomes a means of arrest far more than a means of advance in thought."

23. *Pragmatism*, 76: "With her [pragmatism's] criterion of the practical differences that theories make, we see that she must equally abjure absolute monism and absolute pluralism."

24. Quoted in *The Meaning of Truth*, 79.

25. See Aron Gurwitsch, *Théorie du champ de la conscience* (Paris: Desclée de Brouwer, 1957), 50–52, 109. This work constitutes one of the most thorough studies of James's psychology.

26. *Essays in Radical Empiricism*, 22–23: "Ordinary empiricism, in spite of the fact that conjunctive and disjunctive relations present themselves as being fully coordinate parts of experience, has always shown a tendency to do away with the connexions of things, and to insist most on the disjunctions."

27. Jean André Wahl, *Vers le concret: Études d'histoire de la philosophie contemporaine* (Paris: Vrin, 1936), 5.

28. *Essays in Radical Empiricism*, 40: "It is therefore not a formal question, but a question of empirical fact solely, whether, when you and I are said to know the 'same' Memorial Hall, our minds do terminate at or in a numerically identical percept. Obviously, as a plain matter of fact, they do *not*. . . . You may be on one side of it and I on another."

29. *Principles of Psychology*, 231.

30. *Essays in Radical Empiricism*, 33n6: "Around all the nuclei of shared 'reality' floats the vast cloud of experiences that are wholly subjective, that are non-substitutional, that find not even an eventual ending for themselves in the perceptual world—the mere day-dreams and joys and sufferings and wishes of the individual minds. These exist *with* one another, indeed, and with the objective nuclei, but out of them it is probable that to all eternity no inter-related system of any kind will ever be made."

31. *Essays in Radical Empiricism*, 41: "Do our minds have no object in common after all? Yes, they certainly have *space* in common."

32. *Psychology: Briefer Course*, in *The Works of William James*, 177.

33. *A Pluralistic Universe*, 115.

34. *Pragmatism*, 73: "It is neither a universe pure and simple nor a multiverse pure and simple."

35. For an inventory of all these types of unity and a critique of them, see *Pragmatism*, chapter 4.

36. *A Pluralistic Universe*, 51.

37. *Pragmatism*, 66–67. Emphasis in original.

38. *Pragmatism*, 68.

39. *Pragmatism*, 67. Emphasis in original.

40. *Pragmatism*, 67: "The result is innumerable little hangings-together of the world's parts within the larger hangings-together, little worlds, not only of discourse but of operation, within the wider universe."

41. *Pragmatism*, 76–77.

42. *Pragmatism*, 66: "The parts of our universe *hang together*, instead of being like detached grains of sand." And subsequently, "The world is one just so far as its parts hang together by any definite connexion" (76).

43. *A Pluralistic Universe*, 121.

44. Gabriel Tarde, *Social Laws: An Outline of Sociology*, trans. Howard C. Warren (London: Macmillan, 1899), 178–79.

45. *A Pluralistic Universe*, 147: "The recognition of this fact of coalescence of next with next in concrete experience, so that all the insulating cuts we make there are artificial products of the conceptualizing faculty."

46. *Pragmatism*, 73: "The oneness of things, superior to their manyness, you think must also be more deeply true, must be the more real aspect of the world. The pragmatic view, you are sure, gives us a universe imperfectly rational. The real universe must form an unconditional unit of being, something consolidated, with its parts co-implicated through and through."

47. Gilbert Maire, *William James et le pragmatisme religieux* (Paris: Denoel and Steele, 1933), 159. For an account of knowledge as archipelago and the world as patchwork, see too the passages in Gilles Deleuze on prolongations of Herman Melville through the pragmatism of James and Royce in *Essays Critical and Clinical*, trans. Daniel W. Smith and Michael A. Greco (New York: Verso, 1998), 110–11.

48. *Essays in Radical Empiricism*, 22: "It is essentially a mosaic philosophy, a philosophy of plural facts, like that of Hume and his descendants, who refer these facts neither to substances in which they inhere nor to an absolute mind that creates them as its objects."

49. *Pragmatism*, 67: "They [definite networks] are superposed upon each other; and between them all they let no individual elementary part of the universe escape."

50. *Some Problems of Philosophy*, 69.

51. *Essays in Radical Empiricism*, 27.

52. *The Meaning of Truth*, 98.

53. *The Meaning of Truth*, 201: "*To know an object is here to lead to it through a context which the world supplies.*" Emphasis in original.

54. *The Meaning of Truth*, 80–81.

55. *Essays in Radical Empiricism*, 36: "So the notion of a knowledge still *in transitu* and on its way joins hands here with that notion of a 'pure experience' which I tried to explain."

56. *The Meaning of Truth*, 82.

57. *The Meaning of Truth*, 81. Emphasis mine.

58. *Essays in Radical Empiricism*, 42.

59. *The Meaning of Truth*, 66: "As a matter of fact, and in a general way, the paths that run through conceptual experiences . . . are highly advantageous paths

to follow. Not only do they yield inconceivably rapid transitions; but, owing to the 'universal' character which they frequently possess, and to their capacity for association with one another in great systems, they outstrip the tardy consecutions of the things themselves, and sweep us on towards our ultimate termini in a far more labor-saving way than the following of trains of sensible perception ever could. Wonderful are the new cuts and the short-circuits the thought-paths make."

60. *The Meaning of Truth*, 67: "The key to this difficulty lies in the distinction between knowing as verified and completed, and the same knowing as in transit and on its way."

61. *The Meaning of Truth*, 134: "We throw our concept forward, get a foothold on the consequence, hitch our line to this, and draw our percept up, traveling thus with a hop, skip and jump over the surface of life at a vastly rapider rate than if we merely waded through the thickness of the particulars as accident rained them down upon our heads." A fine theory of consolidation can also be found in Eugène Dupréel's *Essais pluralistes* (Paris: Presses Universitaires de France, 1946), starting on 264. Dupréel develops a theory of convention as consolidation at the same time.

62. See Cicero, *Premiers académiques, Lucullus*, ed. M. Nisard (Paris : Dubochet, 1840), 3:145.

63. *The Meaning of Truth*, 53: "The *ensemble* of perceptions thus thought of as either actual or possible form a system which it is obviously advantageous to us to get into a stable and consistent shape."

64. James uses this phrase in a letter to Nathaniel Southgate Shaler, July 6, 1901 (*Correspondence*, 9:514).

65. A book well worth consulting on this topic is that of Nels Anderson, *The Hobo: The Sociology of the Homeless Man* (1923; Midway reprint, Chicago: University of Chicago, 1975). Significantly, a former hobo wrote this book in 1923, at the request of the School of Urban Sociology of Chicago. On the Chicago School, Ulf Hannerz's extensive overview is worth consulting: *Exploring the City: Inquiries toward an Urban Anthropology* (New York: Columbia University Press, 1980).

66. Anderson describes Hobohemia as follows in *The Hobo*: "The veteran of the road finds other veterans; the old man finds the aged; the chronic grouch finds friendship; the radical, the optimist, the crook, the inebriate, all find others here to tune in with them" (4).

67. Anderson reminds us of this fact in his introduction to *The Hobo*, referring to "the French authority who invented the term 'dromomania'" (xvii), and later in the book writing, "It comes upon us unaware; and often we cut away and go. There are automobiles, railway cars, steamships, airplanes—serving little other purpose, really, than the gratification of wander tendencies" (82).

68. Anderson, *The Hobo*, xviii. Recall that the term "frontier" (and frontier spirit) refers to the progressive conquest of the American West.

1. See Max H. Fisch, "Alexander Bain and the Genealogy of Pragmatism," *Journal of the History of Ideas* 15, no. 3 (1954): 413–44.

2. *Pragmatism*, 99.

3. *The Will to Believe*, 76: "Faith is the readiness to act in a cause the prosperous issue of which is not certified to us in advance."

4. *Varieties of Religious Experience*, 398: "This readiness for great things, and this sense that the world by its importance, wonderfulness, etc., is apt for their production, would seem to be the undifferentiated germ of all the higher faiths."

5. *The Will to Believe*, 80: "Suppose, for example, that I am climbing in the Alps, and have had the ill-luck to work myself into a position from which the only escape is by a terrible leap. Being without similar experience, I have no evidence of my ability to perform it successfully; but hope and confidence in myself make me sure I shall not miss my aim, and nerve my feet to execute what without those subjective emotions would perhaps have been impossible."

6. *The Will to Believe*, 193.

7. *The Will to Believe*, 53: "And often enough our faith beforehand in an uncertified result *is the only thing that makes the result come true.*" Emphasis in original.

8. In a May 6, 1906, letter to Wicenty Lutoslawski, James writes, "Great emergencies and crises show us how much greater our vital resources are than we had supposed" (*Correspondence* 11:220).

9. *The Will to Believe*, 52.

10. *Principles of Psychology*, 926–27: "In certain forms of melancholic perversion of the sensibilities and reactive powers, nothing touches us intimately, rouses us, or wakens natural feeling. The consequence is the complaint so often heard from melancholic patients, that nothing is believed in by them as it used to be, and that all sense of reality is fled from life."

11. *Varieties of Religious Experience*, 135.

12. *Pragmatism*, 44: "In short, she widens the field of search for God. . . . If theological ideas should do this, if the notion of God, in particular, should prove to do it, how could pragmatism possibly deny God's existence?"

13. *Varieties of Religious Experience*, 225: "*Like love or fear*, the faithstate is a natural psychic complex, and carries charity with it by organic consequence. Jubilation is an expansive affection, *and all expansive affections* are self-forgetful and kindly so long as they endure." Emphasis mine.

14. In a letter to Oliver Wendell Holmes, September 17, 1867, James speaks of undergoing such a crisis, speaking of the "deadness of spirit thereby produced" (*Correspondence*, 4:220). And there is a case that his biographers have identified as James's in *Varieties of Religious Experience*:

> "Whilst in this state of philosophic pessimism and general depression of spirits about my prospects, I went one evening into a dressingroom in the twilight to procure some article that was there; when suddenly there fell upon me without any warning . . . a horrible fear of my own existence. Simulta-

neously there arose in my mind the image of an epileptic patient whom I had seen in the asylum, a black-haired youth with greenish skin, entirely idiotic, who used to sit all day on one of the benches, or rather shelves against the wall, with his knees drawn up against his chin. . . . This image and my fear entered into a species of combination with each other. . . . There was such a horror of him, and such a perception of my own merely momentary discrepancy from him, that it was as if something hitherto solid within my breast gave way entirely, and I became a mass of quivering fear. After this the universe was changed for me altogether. . . . I remember wondering how other people could live, how I myself had ever lived, so unconscious of that pit of insecurity beneath the surface of life." (134–35)

Subsequently, James adds: "If I had not clung to scripture-texts . . . I think I should have grown really insane."

15. We also find such an atheist or secular definition of religion in James's correspondence. See James to Edwin Lawrence Godkin, August 17, 1897: "I mean by religion for a man *anything* that for *him* is a live hypothesis in that line, altho it may be a dead one for anyone else" (*Correspondence* 8:294). Emphasis in original.

16. *The Will to Believe*, 32.

17. *Principles of Psychology*, 945: "What is *beyond* the crude experiences is not an *alternative* to them, but something that *means* them for me here and now." Emphasis in original.

18. *Varieties of Religious Experience*, 131.

19. In Dupréel's *Essais pluralistes* may be found a profound reflection on the relation between consistency, convention, and multiplicity, not only from the point of view of the agreement between individuals but also through an examination of the formation of concepts.

20. See David Hume, *Treatise of Human Nature*, ed. L. A. Selby-Bigge (Oxford: Clarendon, 1896), 255: "Two men, who pull the oars of a boat, do it by an agreement or convention, tho' they have never given promises to each other."

21. *Varieties of Religious Experience*, 403.

22. Convention is the only way to understand the apparently contradictory affirmations we find especially in James's correspondence. See, for instance, his reply to a questionnaire from J. B. Pratt in 1904, in which he indicates that he believes in God "more as a powerful ally of my own ideals." See William James, Answers to J. B. Pratt's questionnaire on religion, printed sheet with autograph annotations, 1904, b MS Am 1092.9 (4474), "Religious Experiences," "*Life Is in the Transitions*": *A Web Version of an Exhibition Curated by Linda Simon*, accessed March 14, 2019, https://library.harvard.edu/onlineexhibits/james/religious/6_8 .html; and subsequently, in James to James Henry Leuba, April 17, 1904: "My personal position is simple. I have no living sense of commerce with God" (*Correspondence*, 10:396).

23. Henri Bergson, *The Two Sources of Morality and Religion* (Notre Dame, IN: University of Notre Dame Press, 1977), 22.

24. David Hume, *An Enquiry Concerning the Principles of Morals* (Oxford: Clarendon, 2006), 58–59.

25. *Talks to Teachers on Psychology*, in *The Works of William James*, 33: "Every acquired reaction is, as a rule, either a complication grafted on a native reaction, or a substitute for a native reaction which the same object originally tended to provoke."

26. Dupréel, *Essais pluralistes*, 12.

27. Henri Poincaré, *Science and Hypothesis* (New York: Walter Scott, 1905), 59.

28. Dupréel, *Essais pluralistes*, 75–76.

29. *Varieties of Religious Experience*, 195. Emphasis in original.

30. *Pragmatism*, 45–46.

31. In this respect, James's critiques are much like those of Bergson, even though they do not lead to the same grounds for action. In the first pages of "Life and Consciousness," Bergson writes, "As it [the deductive method] leads him to some very general theory, to an almost empty concept, he can always, later on, place retrospectively in the concept whatever experience has come to teach him of the thing." *Mind-Energy*, trans. H. Wilson Carr (Westport, CT: Greenwood Press, 1975), 5.

32. *Pragmatism*, 107: "When new experiences lead to retrospective judgments, using the past tense, what these judgments utter *was* true, even tho no past thinker had been led there."

33. *A Pluralist Universe*, 61. Emphasis in original.

34. *Pragmatism*, 50–51.

35. *Pragmatism*, 53: "Theism and materialism, so indifferent when taken retrospectively, point, when we take them prospectively, to wholly different outlooks of experience."

36. *Pragmatism*, 62.

37. *The Will to Believe*, 52. And subsequently he writes, "So far as man stands for anything, and is productive or originative at all, his entire vital function may be said to have to deal with maybes" (53).

38. *The Meaning of Truth*, 124–25.

39. *Some Problems of Philosophy*, 73.

40. *A Pluralistic Universe*, 146.

41. *Some Problems of Philosophy*, appendix, 116. Emphasis in original.

42. *Pragmatism*, 44: "But you see already how democratic she [pragmatism] is."

43. *The Meaning of Truth*, 72: "Ethically the pluralistic form of it takes for me a stronger hold on reality than any other philosophy I know of—it being essentially a *social* philosophy, a philosophy of '*co*,' in which conjunctions do the work." James sometimes evokes federalism as a political form of pluralism and opposes it to the monarchist system. Emphasis in original.

44. *Some Problems of Philosophy*, appendix, 115: "The melioristic universe is conceived after a *social* analogy, as a pluralism of independent powers." Emphasis in original.

45. James repeatedly expresses his indebtedness to the French sociologist, notably in *The Will to Believe*, 194n: "Tarde's book (itself a work of genius)." See,

too, *Talks to Teachers*, 38–39: "The moment one hears Tarde's proposition uttered, however, one feels how supremely true it is."

46. Tarde, *Social Laws*, 29.

47. *The Will to Believe*, 19.

48. Recall that James played a leading role in political battles against racism and lynching as well as in the context of the crisis in Venezuela and the war in the Philippines.

49. *The Will to Believe*, 174.

50. Gabriel Tarde, *The Laws of Imitation*, trans. Elsie Clews Parsons (New York: Holt, 1903), 145–46: "Desire and belief: they are the substance and the force, they are the two psychological quantities which are found at the bottom of all the *sensational* qualities with which they combine." Emphasis in original.

51. *The Will to Believe*, 18–19.

52. Tarde, *Laws of Imitation*, 87.

53. On this topic, we may once again see parallels between James and Hume. For an account of sympathy in Hume and his criticism of the other as alter ego, see the excellent article by F. Brahmi, "Sympathie et individualité dans la philosophie politique de David Hume," *Revue philosophique* 182, no. 2 (1992): 211–15.

54. *The Will to Believe*, 29. Emphasis mine.

55. *The Will to Believe*, 29.

56. Jean-Jacques Rousseau. *Du Contrat social; ou, Principes du droit politique* (Paris: Librairie de la Bibliothèque Nationale, 1880) 40.

57. *The Will to Believe*, 194–95.

58. See Émile Durkheim, *Rules of Sociological Method*, trans. W. D. Halls (New York: Free Press, 1982), 54–59.

59. Tarde, *Laws of Imitation*, 34. See Bruno Karsenti's preface to the recent reedition for an account of the opposition between Tarde and Durkheim.

60. James to Sarah Wyman Whitman, June 7, 1899 (*Correspondence* 8:546).

61. *The Meaning of Truth*, 29–30.

62. Josiah Royce, *The Problem of Christianity*, vol. 2, *The Real World and Christian Ideas*, in *The Works of Josiah Royce*, compiled and edited by Mark C. Rooks, electronic ed. (Charlottesville, VA: InteLex, 2004), 2:150.

63. Royce, *Problem of Christianity*, 2:247.

64. Moses Judah Aronson, *La philosophie morale de Josiah Royce* (Paris: Alcan, 1927), 144.

65. Henry James to Grace Norton, July 28, 1883. In Henry James, *The Letters of Henry James*, ed. Percy Lubbock (New York: Scribner's, 1920), 101.

66. As Robert Park writes, "The processes of segregation establish moral distances which make the city a mosaic of little worlds which touch but do not interpenetrate. This makes it possible for individuals to pass quickly and easily from one moral milieu to another, and encourages the fascinating but dangerous experiment of living at the same time in several different contiguous, but otherwise widely separated, worlds." *Human Communities* (Glencoe, IL: Free Press, 1952), cited in Hannerz, *Exploring the City*, 26. This was also a constant theme in

the novelistic work of Henry James, to show how communities based on interest or sympathy were formed or disbanded, as in *The Awkward Age*: "not a formal association nor a secret society—still less a 'dangerous gang' or an organisation for any definite end. We're simply a collection of natural affinities' . . . meeting perhaps principally in Mrs. Brook's drawing-room" (95). Henry James, *The Awkward* Age (New York: Scribner's, 1922), 124.

CONCLUSION

1. Richard Rorty, "Solidarity or Objectivity?" in *Relativism: Interpretation and Confrontation*, ed. Michael Krausz (Notre Dame, IN: University of Notre Dame Press, 1989), 169. See, too, the afterword by Cornell West to *Post-Analytic Philosophy*, eds. John Rachjman and Cornell West (New York: Columbia University Press, 1985).

2. See Tiercelin, *La pensée-signe*, 359; *Pragmatism*, 83.

3. Richard Rorty, "Solidarity or Objectivity?" in *Relativism: Interpretation and Confrontation*, ed. Michael Krausz (Notre Dame, IN: University of Notre Dame Press, 1989), 176.

4. *The Will to Believe*, 54.

AFTERWORD

1. Antonio Damasio, *Self Comes to Mind: Constructing the Conscious Brain* (New York: Vintage Books, 2012), 6, 9.

2. James H. Austin, *Zen and the Brain: Toward an Understanding of Meditation and Consciousness* (Cambridge, MA: MIT Press, 1999).

3. William E. Connolly, "The Complexity of Intention," *Critical Inquiry* 37, no. 4 (2011): 792. Connolly addresses James at length in *Neuropolitics: Thinking, Culture, Speed* (Minneapolis: University of Minnesota Press, 2002) and turns to him at key moments in *The Fragility of Things: Self-Organizing Processes, Neoliberal Fantasies, and Democratic Activism* (Durham, NC: Duke University Press, 2013).

4. Adrian Mackenzie, *Wirelessness: Radical Empiricism in Network Cultures* (Cambridge, MA: MIT Press, 2010), 62–63.

5. Anna Munster, *An Aesthesia of Networks: Conjunctive Experience in Art and Technology* (Cambridge, MA: MIT Press, 2013), 8, 11.

6. Munster, *Aesthesia of Networks*, 12.

7. Munster, *Aesthesia of Networks*, 186.

8. Luciana Parisi, *Contagious Architecture: Computation, Aesthetics, and Space* (Cambridge, MA: MIT Press, 2013), 253.

9. Parisi, *Contagious Architecture*, 256. She also suggests that James' model may remain too topological, thus inadequate to an understanding of quantum realities.

10. Connolly, *Fragility of Things*, 154.

11. See chapter 3, this volume.

12. *Varieties*, 12.

13. *Varieties*, 32.

14. *Varieties*, 33.

15. *Varieties*, 14.

16. Wesley Cooper provides a rigorous account of the unity inherent in the two-fold nature of James's thought, which many prior scholars have treated as a simple divide or as contradictory impulses. See *The Unity of William James's Thought* (Nashville, TN: Vanderbilt University Press, 2002).

17. *Varieties*, 13.

18. See his lectures on exceptional states, which were never compiled, edited, and published in definitive form but have been carefully restored by Eugene Taylor as best possible. Eugene Taylor, *William James on Exceptional Mental States: The 1896 Lowell Lectures* (New York: Scribner, 1983).

19. *Varieties*, 210.

20. *Varieties*, 13.

21. *Varieties*, 262, 53.

22. *Varieties*, 52, 53. Emphasis in original.

23. Gilles Deleuze and Félix Guattari, *Anti-Oedipus: Capitalism and Schizophrenia*, trans. Robert Hurley, Mark Seem, and Helen R. Lane (Minneapolis: University of Minnesota Press, 1983), 25.

24. In this section's heading, I am drawing on the conventions of BL, or boys' love, manga and anime in the use of × to characterize the relation between James and Durkheim, between empiricism and rationalism. The × relation is neither entirely one of conflict (against) nor entirely one of agreement (with), but both, implying a relation of intense affective engagement and erotic entanglement.

25. Durkheim, *Pragmatism and Sociology*, 92.

26. *Varieties*, 67.

27. Durkheim, *Pragmatism and Sociology*, 92. Emphasis in the original.

28. *Varieties*, 69.

29. Timothy Mitchell, "The Stage of Modernity," in *Questions of Modernity*, ed. Timothy Mitchell (Minneapolis: University of Minnesota Press, 2000).

30. Timothy Mitchell, *Colonizing Egypt* (Berkeley: University of California Press, 1988).

31. Terry N. Clark, in his introduction to *Gabriel Tarde: On Communication and Social Influence* (Chicago: University of Chicago Press, 1969), gives a fine account of the conflict between Durkheim and Tarde. One debate has been translated: Eduardo Viana Vargas, Bruno Latour, Bruno Karsenti, Frédérique Aït-Touati, and Louise Salmon, "The Debate between Tarde and Durkheim," *Environment and Planning D: Society and Space* 26, no. 5 (2008): 761–77.

32. *Varieties*, 66.

33. *Varieties*, 112.

34. *Varieties*, 112, 113.

35. *Varieties*, 114.

36. *Varieties*, 113. Emphasis in original.

37. See chapter 2, this volume.

38. This point is made explicitly in Eleanor Rosch, Francisco J. Varela, and Evan Thompson, *The Embodied Mind: Cognitive Science and Human Experience* (Cambridge, MA: MIT Press, 1991).

39. *Varieties*, 11.

40. *Varieties*, 25.

41. *Varieties*, 25.

42. *A Pluralistic Universe*, 121; chapter 2, this volume.

43. Émile Durkheim, *The Elementary Forms of Religious Life*, trans. Karen E. Fields (New York: Free Press, 1995), 420.

44. *Varieties*, 336.

45. Durkheim, *Elementary Forms*, 420.

46. Durkheim, *Elementary Forms*, 420.

47. Karen E. Fields citing psychologist Craig Barclay in note 87 of the translator's introduction to Durkheim, *Elementary Forms*, lxviii.

48. Émile Durkheim, *Moral Education: A Study in the Theory and Application of the Sociology of Education* (New York: Free Press of Glencoe, 1961), cited in Robert Nisbet, *The Sociology of Emile Durkheim* (Oxford: Oxford University Press, 1974), 116.

49. *Varieties*, 26.

50. *Varieties*, 40.

51. *Varieties*, 294, 284.

52. *Varieties*, 299.

53. Michel Foucault, "The Subject and Power," *Critical inquiry* 8, no. 4 (1982): 779–80.

54. *Varieties*, 125.

55. Muriel Combes, *Gilbert Simondon and the Philosophy of the Transindividual*, trans. Thomas Lamarre (Cambridge, MA: MIT Press, 2013), 4.

56. *Varieties*, 189.

57. *Varieties*, 189.

58. Chapter 2, this volume.

59. Chapter 2, this volume.

60. *Varieties*, 176n163, 233.

61. *Varieties*, 189.

62. *The Meaning of Truth*, 45.

63. Steven Meyer, *Irresistible Dictation: Gertrude Stein and the Correlations of Writing and Science* (Stanford, CA: Stanford University Press, 2001), 244.

64. *Varieties*, 338.

65. *Varieties*, 176n163, 233.

66. *Varieties*, 189.

67. *Varieties*, 20.

68. *Varieties*, 241.

69. See Brian Massumi's account of semblance in *Semblance and Event: Activist Philosophy and the Occurrent Arts* (Cambridge, MA: MIT Press, 2011), 15–16, 43–45.

70. Deleuze and Guattari, *Anti-Oedipus*, 42

71. *Varieties*, 211, 262.

72. Donald F. Duclow, "William James, Mind-Cure, and the Religion of Healthy-Mindedness," *Journal of Religion and Health* 41, no. 1 (2002): 45.

73. Duclow, "William James, Mind-Cure," 46–47. See, too, Emma Kate Sutton, "Interpreting 'Mind-Cure': William James and the 'Chief Task . . . of the Science of Human Nature.'" *Journal of the History of the Behavioral Sciences* 48, no. 2 (2012): 115–33.

74. *Varieties*, 78–79.

75. *Varieties*, 79.

76. *Varieties*, 90.

77. Joan Richardson, *A Natural History of Pragmatism* (Cambridge: Cambridge University Press, 2007), 105.

78. *Varieties*, 83–84, 88.

79. *Varieties*, 89. James cites some scattered passages from R. W. Trine, *In Tune with the Infinite* (New York: 26th Thousand, 1897).

80. *Varieties*, 93.

81. *Varieties*, 103.

82. *Varieties*, 114.

83. *Varieties*, 93.

84. In the chapter "William James' Moral Equivalents," Rebecca Solnit provides a fine account of how James discovered that he could not live in a utopic community, which made him reconsider the question of strife and discord, in *A Paradise Built in Hell: The Extraordinary Communities that Arise in Disasters* (New York: Viking, 2009).

85. Erin Manning captures a perfectly Simondonian and Jamesian sense of the potential for ecological practices and thinking through neurodiversity: "What neurodiversity teaches us, it seems to me, are techniques to become attuned to this more-than, to become attuned to the ineffable amodality of experience that activates the contours of the event toward a moving, an encountering, a being-moved in a complex ecology of practices." *Always More than One: Individuation's Dance* (Durham, NC: Duke University Press, 2013), 132.

86. Charles Taylor, *Varieties of Religion Today: William James Revisited* (Cambridge, MA: Harvard University Press, 2002), 43, 46, and 58.

87. Taylor, *Varieties of Religion Today*, 59.

88. Taylor, *Varieties of Religion Today*, 97.

89. Taylor, *Varieties of Religion Today*, 88, 101.

90. Taylor, *Varieties of Religion Today*, 112.

91. Michel Foucault, "Truth and Power: An Interview with Alessandro Fontano and Pasquale Pasquino," in *Power/Knowledge: Selected Interviews and Other Writings, 1972–1977* (New York: Pantheon, 1980), 121.

92. *Pragmatism*, 76–77.

93. See Brian Massumi on the concept "superposition" in *The Power at the End of the Economy* (Durham, NC: Duke University Press, 2015), 11–12.

94. Massumi, *Semblance and Event*, 21.

Bibliography

Anderson, Nels. *The Hobo: The Sociology of the Homeless Man.* 1923. Midway reprint. Chicago: University of Chicago, 1975.

Aronson, Moses Judah. *La philosophie morale de Josiah Royce.* Paris: Alcan, 1927.

Austin, James H. *Zen and the Brain: Toward an Understanding of Meditation and Consciousness.* Cambridge, MA: MIT Press, 1999.

Benmakhlouf, Ali. *Bertrand Russell, L'atomisme logique.* Philosophie 70. Paris: Presses Universitaires de France, 1996.

Benveniste, Émile. *Problèmes de linguistique générale.* Tome I. Paris: Gallimard, 1966.

Bergson, Henri. *Matter and Memory.* Translated by N. M. Paul and W. S. Palmer. New York: Zone Books, 1988.

Bergson, Henri. "Mélanges." Translated by Melissa McMahon. In *Henri Bergson: Key Writings*, edited by Keith Ansell Pearson and John Mullarkey. New York: Continuum, 2002.

Bergson, Henri. *Mind-Energy.* Translated by H. Wilson Carr. Westport, CT: Greenwood Press, 1975.

Bergson, Henri. *Sur le pragmatisme de William James.* Edited by Stéphane Madelrieux. Paris: Presses Universitaires de France, 2011.

Bergson, Henri. *The Two Sources of Morality and Religion.* Notre Dame, IN: University of Notre Dame Press, 1977.

Brahmi, F. "Sympathie et individualité dans la philosophie politique de David Hume." *Revue philosophique* 182, no. 2 (1992): 201–27.

Chauviré, Christiane. *Peirce et la signification: Introduction à la logique du vague.* Paris: Presses Universitaires de France, 1995.

Cicéron. *Premiers académiques, Lucullus.* Edited by M. Nisard. Tome III. Paris: Dubochet, 1840.

Clark, Terry N. *Gabriel Tarde: On Communication and Social Influence.* Chicago: University of Chicago Press, 1969.

Combes, Muriel. *Gilbert Simondon and the Philosophy of the Transindividual.* Translated by Thomas Lamarre. Cambridge, MA: MIT Press, 2013.

Connolly, William E. "The Complexity of Intention." *Critical Inquiry* 37, no. 4 (2011): 791–98.

Connolly, William E. *The Fragility of Things: Self-Organizing Processes, Neoliberal Fantasies, and Democratic Activism.* Durham, NC: Duke University Press, 2013.

Connolly, William E. *Neuropolitics: Thinking, Culture, Speed.* Minneapolis: University of Minnesota Press, 2002.

Cooper, Wesley. *The Unity of William James's Thought.* Nashville, TN: Vanderbilt University Press, 2002.

Damasio, Antonio. *Self Comes to Mind: Constructing the Conscious Brain.* New York: Vintage Books, 2012.

Deledalle, Gérard. Afterword to *Écrits sur le signe*, by Charles Sanders Peirce. Paris: Éditions du Seuil, 1978.

Deledalle, Gérard. *La philosophie américaine.* Lausanne: De Boeck University, 1983.

Deleuze, Gilles. *Difference and Repetition.* Translated by Paul Patton. New York: Columbia University Press, 1994.

Deleuze, Gilles. *Essays Critical and Clinical.* Translated by Daniel W. Smith and Michael A. Greco. New York: Verso, 1998.

Deleuze, Gilles. *The Logic of Sense.* Translated by Mark Lester. London: Athlone Press, 1990.

Deleuze, Gilles, and Félix Guattari. *Anti-Oedipus: Capitalism and Schizophrenia.* Translated by Robert Hurley, Mark Seem, and Helen R. Lane. Minneapolis: University of Minnesota Press, 1983.

Deleuze, Gilles, and Félix Guattari. *What Is Philosophy?* Translated by Hugh Tomlinson and Graham Burchell. New York: Columbia University Press, 1994.

Duclow, Donald F. "William James, Mind-Cure, and the Religion of Healthy-Mindedness." *Journal of Religion and Health* 41, no. 1 (2002): 45–56.

Dufrenne, Mikel. *La notion d'a priori.* Paris: Presses Universitaires de France, 1959.

Dupréel, Eugène. *Essais pluralistes.* Paris: Presses Universitaires de France, 1946.

Durkheim, Émile. *The Elementary Forms of Religious Life.* Translated by Karen E. Fields. New York: Free Press, 1995.

Durkheim, Émile. *Moral Education: A Study in the Theory and Application of the Sociology of Education.* New York: Free Press of Glencoe, 1961.

Durkheim, Émile. *Pragmatism and Sociology.* Translated by J. C. Whitehouse. Cambridge: Cambridge University Press, 1983.

Durkheim, Émile. *Rules of Sociological Method.* Translated by W. D. Halls. New York: Free Press, 1982.

Emerson, Ralph Waldo. *The Collected Works of Ralph Waldo Emerson.* Electronic edition. Charlottesville, VA: InteLex, 2008. Based on *The Collected Works of Ralph Waldo Emerson*, edited by Alfred R. Ferguson, Jean Ferguson Carr, and Douglas Emory Wilson. 7 vols. Cambridge, MA: The Belknap Press of Harvard University Press, 1971–2007.

Fisch, Max H. "Alexander Bain and the Genealogy of Pragmatism." *Journal of the History of Ideas* 15, no. 3 (1954): 413–44.

Foucault, Michel. "The Subject and Power." *Critical Inquiry* 8, no. 4 (1982): 777–95.

Foucault, Michel. "Truth and Power: An Interview with Alessandro Fontano and Pasquale Pasquino." In *Power/Knowledge: Selected Interviews and Other Writings, 1972–1977*, 109–33. New York: Pantheon, 1980.

Gurwitsch, Aron. *Théorie du champ de la conscience.* Paris: Desclée de Brouwer, 1957.

Hannerz, Ulf. *Exploring the City: Inquiries toward an Urban Anthropology.* New York: Columbia University Press, 1980.

Horkheimer, Max. *The Eclipse of Reason.* New York: Continuum, 1992.

Hume, David. *An Enquiry Concerning Human Understanding.* Toronto: Broadview, 2011.

Hume, David. *An Enquiry Concerning the Principles of Morals.* Oxford: Clarendon, 2006.

Hume, David. *Treatise of Human Nature.* Edited by L. A. Selby-Bigge. Oxford: Clarendon, 1896.

Husserl, Edmund. *Cartesian Meditations.* Translated by Dorion Cairns. The Hague: Martinus Nijhoff, 1960.

James, Henry. *The Awkward Age.* New York: Scribner's, 1922.

James, Henry. *The Letters of Henry James.* Edited and selected by Percy Lubbock. New York: Scribner's, 1920.

James, William. *The Correspondence of William James.* Electronic edition. Charlottesville, VA: InteLex, 2008. Based on *The Correspondence of William James*, edited by Ignas K. Skrupskelis and Elizabeth M. Berkeley, with Bernice Grohskopf and Wilma Bradbeer, 12 vols. Charlottesville: University Press of Virginia, 1992–2004.

James, William. *The Works of William James.* Electronic edition. Charlottesville, VA: InteLex, 2008. Based on *The Works of William James*, edited by Frederick H. Burkhardt, Fredson Bowers, and Ignas K. Skrupskelis, 19 vols. Cambridge, MA: Harvard University Press, 1975–88.

Kant, Immanuel. "On a Newly Arisen Superior Tone in Philosophy." In *Raising the Tone of Philosophy*, edited and translated by Peter Fenves, 51–81. Baltimore, MD: Johns Hopkins University Press, 1993.

Lapoujade, David. *Aberrant Movements: The Philosophy of Gilles Deleuze.* Translated by Joshua David Jordan. Semiotext(e) Foreign Agents Series. Cambridge, MA: MIT Press, 2017.

Lapoujade, David. *Fictions du pragmatisme: William et Henry James.* Paris: Les Éditions du minuit, 2008.

Lapoujade, David. *Power of Time / Potências do Tempo.* English translation by Andrew Goffey. Sao Paolo: N-1 Publications, 2013.

Leroux, Emmanuel. *Le pragmatisme américain et anglais: Étude historique et critique.* Paris: Alcan, 1922.

Mackenzie, Adrian. *Wirelessness: Radical Empiricism in Network Cultures.* Cambridge, MA: MIT Press, 2010.

Madelrieux, Stéphane, ed. *Bergson et James: Cent an après.* Paris: Presses Universitaires de France, 2011.

Madelrieux, Stéphane. *William James : L'attitude empiriste.* Paris: Presses Universitaires de France, 2008.

Maire, Gilbert. *William James et le pragmatisme religieux*. Paris: Denoel and Steele, 1933.

Manning, Erin. *Always More than One: Individuation's Dance*. Durham, NC: Duke University Press, 2013.

Marcuse, Ludwig. *La philosophie américaine*. Paris: Gallimard, 1967.

Massumi, Brian. *The Power at the End of the Economy*. Durham, NC: Duke University Press, 2015.

Massumi, Brian. *Semblance and Event: Activist Philosophy and the Occurrent Arts*. Cambridge, MA: MIT Press, 2011.

Meyers, Steven. *Irresistible Dictation: Gertrude Stein and the Correlations of Writing and Science*. Stanford, CA: Stanford University Press, 2001.

Mitchell, Timothy. *Colonizing Egypt*. Berkeley: University of California Press, 1988.

Mitchell, Timothy. "The Stage of Modernity." In *Questions of Modernity*, edited by Timothy Mitchell, 1–34. Minneapolis: University of Minnesota Press, 2000.

Munster, Anna. *An Aesthesia of Networks: Conjunctive Experience in Art and Technology*. Cambridge, MA: MIT Press, 2013.

Nisbet, Robert. *The Sociology of Emile Durkheim*. Oxford: Oxford University Press, 1974.

Parisi, Luciana. *Contagious Architecture: Computation, Aesthetics, and Space*. Cambridge, MA: MIT Press, 2013.

Park, Robert. *Human Communities*. Glencoe, IL: Free Press, 1952.

Peirce, Charles Sanders. *The Collected Papers of Charles Sanders Peirce*. Electronic ed. Charlottesville, VA: InteLex, 1994. Based on *The Collected Papers of Charles Sanders Peirce*. Vols. 1-6, edited by Charles Hartshorne and Paul Weiss; vols. 7-8 edited by A. W. Burks. Cambridge: Belknap Press of Harvard University Press, 1958–66.

Peirce, Charles Sanders. *The Writings of Charles S. Peirce—A Chronological Edition*. Electronic edition. Charlottesville, VA: InteLex, 2003. Based on *The Writings of Charles S. Peirce—A Chronological Edition*, edited by Max H. Fisch, Edward C. Moore, and Nathan Houser. Bloomington: Peirce Edition Project, Indiana University Press, 1976–99.

Poincaré, Henri. *Science and Hypothesis*. New York: Walter Scott, 1905.

Richardson, Joan. *A Natural History of Pragmatism*. Cambridge: Cambridge University Press, 2007.

Rorty, Richard. "Solidarity or Objectivity?" In *Relativism: Interpretation and Confrontation*, edited by Michael Krausz, 5–6. Notre Dame, IN: University of Notre Dame Press, 1989.

Rosch, Eleanor, Francisco J. Varela, and Evan Thompson. *The Embodied Mind: Cognitive Science and Human Experience*. Cambridge, MA: MIT Press, 1991.

Rousseau, Jean-Jacques. *Du Contrat social; ou, Principes du droit politique*. Paris: Librairie de la Bibliothèque Nationale, 1880.

Royce, Josiah. *The Works of Josiah Royce*. Compiled and edited by Mark C. Rooks. Electronic edition. 13 vols. Charlottesville, VA: InteLex, 2004.

Russell, Bertrand. "As a European Radical Sees It." *Freeman* 4 (March 8, 1922): 610.

Russell, Bertrand. *My Philosophical Development*. London: Allen and Unwin, 1959.

Sartre, Jean-Paul. *La transcendence de l'ego*. Paris: Vrin, 1966.

Schneider, Hubert W. *A History of American Philosophy*. New York: Columbia University Press, 1946.

Schelling, F. W. J. "Exposé de l'empirisme philosophique." *Philosophie*, no. 40 (1993): 4–23.

Smith, John E. Introduction to *The Varieties of Religious Experience*, by William James. Cambridge, MA: Harvard University Press, 1985.

Solnit, Rebecca. *A Paradise Built in Hell: The Extraordinary Communities that Arise in Disasters*. New York: Viking, 2009.

Stengers, Isabelle. *Thinking with Whitehead: A Free and Wild Creation of Concepts*. Translated by Michael Chase. Cambridge, MA: Harvard University Press, 2011.

Sutton, Emma Kate. "Interpreting 'Mind-Cure': William James and the 'Chief Task . . . of the Science of Human Nature.'" *Journal of the History of the Behavioral Sciences* 48, no. 2 (2012): 115–33.

Tarde, Gabriel. *The Laws of Imitation*. Translated by Elsie Clews Parsons. New York: Holt, 1903.

Tarde, Gabriel. *Social Laws: An Outline of Sociology*. Translated by Howard C. Warren. London: Macmillan, 1899.

Taylor, Charles. *Varieties of Religion Today: William James Revisited*. Cambridge, MA: Harvard University Press, 2002.

Taylor, Eugene. *William James on Exceptional Mental States: The 1896 Lowell Lectures*. New York: Scribner, 1983.

Tiercelin, Claudine. *La pensée-signe: Études sur C. S. Peirce*. Nîmes: J. Chambon, 1993.

Trine, R. W. *In Tune with the Infinite*. New York: 26th Thousand, 1897.

Viana Vargas, Eduardo, Bruno Latour, Bruno Karsenti, Frédérique Aït-Touati, and Louise Salmon. "The Debate between Tarde and Durkheim." *Environment and Planning D: Society and Space* 26, no. 5 (2008): 761–77.

Wahl, Jean André. *Vers le concret: Études d'histoire de la philosophie contemporaine*. Paris: Vrin, 1936.

West, Cornell. "Afterword: The Politics of American Neo-Pragmatism." In *Post-Analytic Philosophy*, edited by John Rachjman and Cornell West. New York: Columbia University Press, 1985.

Index

absolutism, 61–62
abstractionism, 31
accidents, 89
action: in crises, 52, 129n8; and faith, 52–53, 56, 129n3; and ideas, 48–49, 55–56, 101–2; and informal philosophies, 59; and James's pragmatism, 2, 5; and open worlds, 62; and pragmatic truth, 35–36, 61; and religion, 55, 57; the series problem, 49; theoretical/practical distinction, 59–60
adaptionism, 98
Anderson, Nels, 128nn65–68
Austin, James H., 77

Bain, Alexander, 61
belief: absences of, 53; admissibility of, 111–14; in civilization, 86; as construction, 44; definitions of, 51–52; determining of, 21; and emotions, 22, 28; and faith, 52, 129n4; and melancholy, 53, 129n11; prestige and, 65–66; and religion, 54; right to, 113–14; roles of, 61; as semiotic process, 20; and series, 44; and shocks, 21, 44; social, 65–67, 69; and truth, 28–29
Bergson, Henri: on deduction, 131n31; and foundational subjects, 15; on habit, 57; images, 14, 122n13; influence on James, 14, 83, 122n10, 122n12; and pure experience, 16; on reality outside consciousness, 17, 121n8
blank slates, 9–10

capitalism, 1–2, 47
Cartesianism, 9–11, 23, 25
civilization, 86, 92–93, 117

closed worlds, 62–63
common sense, 65
communities of interpretation, 63, 66, 70–71
community. *See* society
concepts: conventional capacity of, 25; as conventions, 58; definitions of, 34, 46, 128n61; importance of consequences, 125n13; inherent practicality, 59–60; and intermediary series, 46, 127n59; and perceptions, 46, 128n63. *See also* knowledge
Connolly, William, 78–79, 133n3
consciousness: continuities and discontinuities of, 38–39; definition of, 3; and faith, 53–54; fields of, 7, 18, 23, 102, 124n42; functional aspects of, 24–26; makeup of, 13; philosophies beginning with, 43; and pure experience, 10–14, 17; and relations, 41–42; and religion, 56–57; and religion-science relationship, 95; and resemblance, 28; sense of futurity, 125n15; and signs, 7–8, 22; streams of, 1, 16, 37–38, 46, 57, 65, 126n30; and truth of ideas, 31. *See also* psychology; *Principles of Psychology*
consensus, 74–75
consistency, 41–42
continuities, 38–39, 126n28, 126n31
conventionalism, 58
conventions: and communities of interpretation, 63–64; and consensus, 74; definitions of, 56, 69; functional, 25–26; Hume's oarsmen example, 130n20; perceptions as, 57; pragmatism evaluating, 59; religious, 57, 130n22; and rules, 58–59; in society, 63–64, 66–67, 69–70

conversation, 1–2, 74–75
conversion, 54–55, 82
Cooper, Wesley, 134n16
crystallization, 13, 91, 100–103, 109–10

Damasio, Antonio, 77, 79, 84
Darwinism, 5, 69, 92, 107
Deleuze, Gilles, 83, 122n17
Dewey, John, 1–2, 63–64, 68, 73
dirty regions, 94, 97, 103, 116
disjunctions, 37, 39
dispositions, 112–13, 117
diversity: individuals, 103–4; and evil, 110; natural, 80–81, 92, 118; neurodiversity, 111, 136n85; and pluralism, 92
doubt, 25
Dupréel, Eugène, 58, 128n61, 130n19
Durkheim, Émile, 68, 84–86, 92, 94–97, 122n16
Durkheimian eras, 112–13

ecological thinking, 99, 111, 118
education, 57–58, 65, 131n25
Emerson, Ralph Waldo, 5, 120n9, 121n11
emotions, 20–22, 28, 53, 106–8
the empirical, 15, 123n18
empiricism, classical, 9–10, 37
energetic models, 100–102, 104, 108, 111, 116
epistemology, 47–48, 69
ethnocentrism, 75
events, 15, 17–19, 20–21
evil, 88, 110
evolutionary theory, 92–93, 98–99, 107–8
exceptional states, 81–82, 105, 109, 111, 134n18
experience, 15

faith, 4–7, 52–56, 62–67, 70, 73, 75, 129nn3–5, 129n7
flows: of beliefs, 59, 65; of consciousness, 7–8, 16, 31, 38–39, 53, 57, 65; and crises of faith, 54; and environmental determinants, 116; hobos as, 47; infraindividual, 68; knowledge as, 46; of life, 3, 15; material, 16, 22, 91–94, 97, 99, 109, 111; matter and, 3, 14, 104; of thought, 3, 28, 59, 61; of time, 17, 38–39; of the world, 2, 42
forms: elementary, 92, 96–97; functions and, 23; Husserl and, 16; Kant and, 16, 123n21;

and material, 16–17, 36, 48; as nonconstitutive, 23–24; psychological, 11, 16, 91, 99, 104, 112; in pure experience, 23; and radical empiricism, 94; religious, 112–13; varieties and, 92
Foucault, Michel, 97, 113–15, 117
fruits. See roots and fruits
functions, 23–28, 91–92, 117

Green, Thomas Hill, 37
groundlessness, 99, 112
Guattari, Félix, 83, 105, 122n17, 123

happiness, 107–8
healthy-mindedness, 87–88, 106–7
Hegel, Georg Wilhelm Friedrich, 120n9
Hegelianism: Anglo-Saxon, 120n9; emphasis on disjunctions, 37; God and reason in, 88; James and, 2, 39, 73; monism of, 39–40, 88
hobos, 47, 128nn65–67
Horkeimer, Max, 1
Hume, David, 9, 57, 68, 130n20
Husserl, Edmund, 11, 16, 24–25, 91, 123n20

ideas, 27–35, 47–49, 54–55, 60, 125n17.
    See also truth
ignorance, 24
immanent variation, 80, 98–99, 103, 110–11, 116
imperialism, 86
individualism, 79–81, 84–85, 87, 90–92
individuals, 64–65, 79–81, 84, 89–94, 97–98, 103–5, 116
individuation, 100–104, 106, 109, 116
instincts, 57–58, 131n25
interpretation, 18, 44

James, Henry, 70, 132n66
James, Henry, Sr., 5
James, William: career overview, 120n5; crisis of faith, 121n12, 129n14; criticism of the United States, 2, 119n3; lecture composition strategy, 89–90; legacy of, 1; politics of, 132n48; and religion, 54, 59, 130n22
James, William, philosophy of, 11–12, 42, 48: communities of interpretation, 70–71; contemporary applications of, 77–79, 86, 115–17; as ecological, 99, 111; historical con-

texts, 73–75, 112–13; and isomorphism, 90; and the natural sciences, 80, 91–93, 104, 107–8; reality of desire, 83; and relations, 79; self in, 84; subjectivity in, 98

Kant, Immanuel, 11, 16, 43, 83–84, 91, 123n21
knowledge, 43–49, 127n55, 128n60. *See also* concepts

leaps, 43–46, 52, 129n5
lines, 39–43
little absolutes, 102, 111, 113
little worlds, 41

MacKenzie, Adrian, 78
Manning, Erin, 136n85
massive modernity thesis, 97, 115, 117
Massumi, Brian, 117
material, 12–13, 16–17, 22–25
material flows, 91
materialism, 60–61, 131n35
mechanization, 104–5
media studies, 78–80, 87, 115–17
medical materialism, 104, 107
meliorism, 63, 107
Meyer, Steven, 102
milieus, 100–103, 109, 116
mind-cure movement, 106–11, 114
Mitchell, Timothy, 86
modernity, 111–13
monism, 10, 13–17, 37, 39–40, 121n7, 126n23
mosaic philosophy, 42, 71, 127n48
multiplicity, 42, 127n46
Munster, Anna, 78

naïveté, 5, 11, 24–25, 55
natural diversity, 80–81, 92, 118
natural sciences: and consciousness, 81; and empiricism, 107, 115; and evolution, 99; and individualism, 80, 91–92, 104; and material flows, 91, 93; and the mind-cure movement, 108; and religion, 95; and social sciences, 104; and subjectivity, 98
neo-pragmatism, 1–2, 73–74
networks, 40, 42–43, 47, 127n47
neurodiversity, 111, 136n85
Nietzsche, Friedrich, 5, 25
nihilism, 54–55

objects: consciousness of, 10–12; contexts of, 44, 127n53; as convention, 25; and experiences, 13–14, 22, 91; and ideas, 28; knowledge of, 43–44, 46, 51; object-functions, 23; in Peirce's semiotics, 19; of religious belief, 54–55; Schelling on, 123n18; understanding, 97. *See also* roots and fruits; subjects: and objects
open worlds, 62–63
optimism, 63
organisms, 103–6

Parisi, Luciana, 78–79, 133n9
Park, Robert, 132n66
Peirce, Charles Sanders: and community, 63, 73; on consensus, 74; and doubt, 25; and James, 3, 19, 120n6; and the real, 124n35; semiotics of, 19, 124n31, 124n43
perception: and concepts, 46; as conventional, 57; and coterminousness of minds, 38; definition of, 21; of events, 20; insufficiency of, 53; lines of, 40; in pragmatism, 32
pessimism, 63
planes of immanence, 80, 99, 104, 122n17. *See also* pure experience; transcendental fields
pluralism: and conventionalism, 58; and diversity, 92; and ethnocentrism, 75; and evil, 88; and healthy-mindedness, 88; and individual faith, 63; and pragmatism, 6–7, 126n21, 126n23; and pure experience, 36; and radical empiricism, 7, 61–62; and rationality, 115; and religious experience, 89; as social philosophy, 63, 131n43; and theism, 87–89
plurality, 36
the pluriverse, 39, 126n34
Poincaré, Henri, 58
possession, 17–18, 19, 123n28
post-Durkheimian era, 112–13
power, 114–16
practice, 33, 35, 48, 61
pragmatism, 1–6; and absolutism, 2, 7, 39; ambitions of, 61; and American capitalism, 1–2, 47; as antitheoretical, 33, 48; as concrete, 33; criticisms of, 29; as democratic, 7; and empiricism, 26–62, 93–94, 97; and epistemology, 47–48; and ethnocentrism, 75; and functions, 26; and hobos, 47;

pragmatism (continued)
    meaning in, 60–61; as method, 3–4, 6, 35, 59, 120n7; and monism, 39; and ordinary people, 75; and philosophy, 59, 61; and pluralism, 6–7; problem of, 7–8, 48; and psychology, 7; and rationalism, 2, 84–87, 134n24; and religious belief, 54, 129n12; thought and consequence in, 33, 125n13; three axes of, 7–8, 48; and transcendentalism, 5, 73
Principles of Psychology, 3, 10–11, 77, 78, 124n39. *See also* psychology
psyches, 100–101, 105, 116
psychic realities, 84
psychology, 7, 83; the body in, 22–23; ego, rejection of, 21–22; emotion in, 20; forms in, 16–17; and futurity, 125n15; ideas in, 31; individual character, 103; and material flows, 16, 91; nonconsciousness, 102; problem of, 8; pure experience in, 10–11. *See also* consciousness; *Principles of Psychology*
pure experience, 3, 9; and empiricism, 9–13; events in, 15, 17–18, 20–21; fabric metaphors, 14, 122n10; forms, as nonconstitutive, 23; and functions, 23–24; interpretations populating, 19–20; as for itself, 15–16; and knowledge, 45, 127n55; and material, 12–14; and personal experience, 104; possession and disappearance of, 17–18, 123n28; in *Principles of Psychology*, 10–12; problems with, 14; and relations, 13–14; and religious institutions, 114; reversal of perspective on, 15–16; as shock, 20–21; subjects, assumptions of, 14–15; Taylor on, 114; and transcendental philosophies, 11, 15. *See also* planes of immanence; transcendental fields

radical empiricism, 3; as antitheoretical, 48; calls for, 122n17; Durkheim on, 122n16; *Essays in Radical Empiricism*, 12; as excavation process, 94; functions and conventions in, 23–26; interpretation and signifying series, 17–23; pluralism of, 7, 61–62; and pragmatism, 26, 62; problem of, 8; pure experience, 9–13; and radical historicism, 115; and rationalism, 87; roots and fruits metaphor, 93–94; and relations,

36–37; vague monism, 13–17; withness, 78–79, 95, 117
rationalism: and civilization, 86, 114; and evil, 88, 110; limits of, 85, 96; and mind-cure movement, 108; new- versus habit-ideas, 34; and pragmatism, 84–87, 134n24; and psychology, 31; resituating of, 115; truth in, 31, 33–34
Rationalization, 115, 117
reality, 20–21, 70, 124nn35–36
regions, 93–98
relations: coalescence, 36–42, 44, 62, 73, 79, 127n45
religion, 54–57: Durkheim and, 95; goals of, 81–82; healthy-mindedness, 87–88, 106–7; and experience, 83–84, 89, 95, 111, 114, 117; as individualistic, 80–81, 84; institutions, 81, 84, 87, 98, 110–14; maladaptation in, 98; and Matthew 7:16, 93–94; and mind-cure, 106–7, 111; and pragmatism, 54, 82–83, 129n12; saints, 97–98, 108, 110–11, 114; and science, 81, 95; sick souls, 87–88, 105–6. *See also The Varieties of Religious Experience*
resemblance, 28, 32–33, 35, 68. *See also* semiotics
Richardson, Joan, 107
roots and fruits metaphor, 41, 44, 93–97, 116
Rorty, Richard, 1–2, 73–75
Rousseau, Jean-Jacques, 67–68
Royce, Josiah, 63, 66, 70, 73
Russell, Bertrand, 28–30, 34, 122n11, 125n5

Sartre, Jean-Paul, 123n20
satisfaction, 29–32, 35, 58–59, 106, 115
Saussure, Ferdinand de, 19, 124n30
Schelling, F. W. J., 123n18
science studies, 79
The Secret of Hegel, 120n9
semiotics, 6, 17–23, 70, 86–87, 124n31, 124n43. *See also* resemblance
signs: as condensed verification, 35; and consciousness, 7; and faith, 6; Peirce's model, 19; de Saussure's model, 19, 124n30; shock as, 21; and thought, 19
Simondon, Gilbert, 100–101, 103, 105, 109–10, 116
social Darwinism, 92, 98
social evolution, 99

CPSIA information can be obtained
at www.ICGtesting.com
Printed in the USA
BVHW031201140520
579656BV00002B/208